JOHN JAMES AUDUBON

EX LIBRIS
MARIA BOWEN CHAPIN
C.S.HALE 1922

Chapin Patrons

John James Audubon

ELLA M. FOSHAY

For the Robertsons,
With best wishes,
Ella Foshay
9/17/97

Harry N. Abrams, Inc., Publishers

IN ASSOCIATION WITH

The National Museum of American Art, Smithsonian Institution

Series Director: Margaret L. Kaplan
Editor: Elaine M. Stainton
Designer: Raymond P. Hooper
Photo Editor: Uta Hoffmann

Library of Congress Cataloging-in-Publication Data

Foshay, Ella M., 1948–
    John James Audubon / Ella M. Foshay.
        p.   cm. — (Library of American art)
    Includes bibliographical references (p.   ) and index.
    ISBN 0–8109–1973–7 (hardcover)
    1. Audubon, John James, 1785–1851.   2. Animal painters—United
States—Biography.   I. National Museum of American Art (U.S.)
II. Title.   III. Series: Library of American art (Harry N. Abrams, Inc.)
QL31.A9F65   1997
598'.092—dc21
[B]   96–50408

Frontispiece:
John Syme. *John James Audubon*. 1826. Oil on canvas,
35½ x 27½". White House Historical Association

Printed and bound in Japan

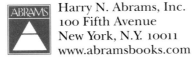 Harry N. Abrams, Inc.
100 Fifth Avenue
New York, N.Y. 10011
www.abramsbooks.com

Contents

Acknowledgments

The wisdom and eloquence of Monique Richards Pettit are imprinted on every page of this book, especially the captions, which are hers more than mine.

To complete this one volume in somewhat less time than it took Audubon to produce his entire oeuvre, I depended upon the advice and support of Gloria Gilda Deák, Barbara Novak, Ninna Denny, Margaret Gordon, Trudy Mollenberg, Vivian Sonnenborn, Cynthia Cook, Tia Powell, David Combs, Robert Rainwater, Mary Le Croy, Miggie Symonds, Carole Slatkin, and Margie Donohue. The staff at Harry N. Abrams, Inc., especially Margaret Kaplan, Uta Hoffman, Elaine Stainton, and Raymond Hooper, provided invaluable help. Finally, a heartfelt thank-you goes to the New York Public Library for giving me a perch in the Frederick Lewis Allen Memorial Room and to Michael, Ella, and Gussie for tending the nest.

Detail of Audubon's watercolor,
Golden Eagle (overleaf)

Golden Eagle

I. Early Life and Work

A diminutive figure of a man in the lower left corner of John James Audubon's magnificent original watercolor of the *Golden Eagle* has been identified by several writers as a self-portrait of the artist (p. 7 and opposite). Here, Audubon has portrayed himself, as an artist-frontiersman, dedicated to the pursuit and understanding of nature. Dressed in buckskin clothes and cap, the indomitable explorer makes his way over a vertiginous chasm between two rocky ledges in an uninhabited mountain landscape. He sits astride a slender, uprooted tree trunk that has been denuded of branches (presumably by the artist, who continues to shave remaining protrusions), and inches himself along to bridge the gap. The broken top of the trunk suggests that it is a thin and weak support for a man carrying a gun and a dead bird strapped to his back. Audubon thus identifies himself as an artist embarked on a dangerous journey that requires courage, skill, and ingenuity to survive. It is an image of heroic pursuit; however, in the context of this plate, it is entirely false. In February 1833, Audubon purchased a live Golden Eagle from the proprietor of the natural history museum in Boston, and, after observing the caged bird in his rooming house quarters in that city, stabbed it through the heart and began to make this painting.

This contradiction between the reality of the painter's experience in making the image and his artistic projection of it typifies the tenuous balance between fact and fiction that runs through John James Audubon's life and work. Lewis Mumford called the artist an "exuberant French coxcomb" who transformed himself into an archetypal American hero by blending the virtues of George Washington, Daniel Boone, and Benjamin Franklin. On one hand, Audubon subscribed to the legend that he was the lost Dauphin of France, son of Louis XVI and Marie Antoinette, plucked out of prison during the Revolution and entrusted to a seaman; on the other, he claimed a mother "of Spanish extraction . . . as beautiful as she was wealthy," who bore him on American soil in the state of Louisiana.[1] Although both of these stories are untrue, they combine to form a true portrait of an artist who indulged in tall tales and whose work encompasses both the idealized style of a French academician and the direct observation of nature embodied in an American Hudson River School drawing.

The contradictory claims of Old and New World heritages served in part to obscure Audubon's real background. Born Jean Rabine on April 26, 1785, he was the illegitimate son of Jean Audubon, a French sea captain, slaver, merchant, and plantation owner, and Jeanne Rabine, a servant girl who died a few months

Golden Eagle

Audubon's name: Golden Eagle. 1833.
Watercolor, pastel, graphite, and selective glazing on paper. 38 × 25½".
Collection of The New-York Historical Society.

Particularly dramatic, even life-threatening, circumstances surrounded the making of this watercolor of the Golden Eagle. In 1833, Audubon purchased a live, caged specimen of this magnificent bird which had been caught in a spring trap set for foxes. He brought the bird home and spent three days observing the eagle. "I occupied myself a whole day in watching his movements; on the next I came to a determination as to the position in which I might best represent him; and," Audubon continued, "on the third thought of how I could take away his life with the least pain." (Ornithological Biography, 2:465)

Working intensively, sometimes day and night, it took Audubon fourteen days to complete this drawing, more than any other except for the Wild Turkey. Audubon represents the eagle with wings spreading in flight as he had admired it near the Bay of Fundy, "launched from the cliff, soaring aloft," and here carrying its Northern Hare prey in its talons. (Journals, 2:431)

after her son's birth. Perhaps in an effort to evoke the fragrant tropical landscape of his real birthplace, Les Cayes, on the southern coast of present-day Haiti, Audubon recalled later in life that he "received breath and life, . . . under the dark foliage of an orange tree, with a load of golden fruit and blossoms upon which fed that airy sylph the Hummingbird."[2] Certainly, his romantic, hot-house prose suggests that from the moment of birth, he was delivered into the warm embrace of nature, which, more than any national birthplace, would remain his spiritual home for the rest of his life.

In 1789, Captain Audubon took his son back to France, where he was raised with kindness by his father's well-to-do wife, Anne Moynet in Brittany, near the coastal town of Nantes. There Audubon led the life of a country gentleman's son. In addition to regular schooling, he acquired finesse in socially-enhancing skills: he learned to play the violin, he studied fencing, and he took dancing lessons. He spent a few years of study at a naval academy in Rochefort-sur-Mer, where Captain Audubon placed him in the hope that his son would follow in his own footsteps in pursuing a maritime career. Jean succeeded admirably at climbing masts, setting sails, shooting, and sailing, but he failed mathematics, and his father was forced to withdraw him from the school.

Throughout his youth in France, Audubon remembered one activity with special pleasure. He loved wandering the countryside, collecting birds' nests and plant specimens, and making drawings of them on his return home. In recognition of his son's pleasure and ability in this pursuit, Captain Audubon gave him illustrated books to copy in order to improve his technique. Audubon claimed that his childhood drawings were almost exclusively of birds and that, since they never met his expectations, he burned all the previous year's work on each birthday.

In 1803, the eighteen-year-old John James was sent by his father to the United States to avoid conscription in Napoleon's burgeoning armies. Captain Audubon wanted his son to take on the responsibility of Mill Grove, a two-hundred-acre farm outside Philadelphia that he had purchased in 1789 and paid for partly with the barter of sugar from his ship's cargo. He had hoped to profit from the purchase by mining deposits of lead. Although a smelting mill was built, the mining enterprise was not successful. Not much interested in property management, the younger Audubon spent most of his time at Mill Grove happily exploring nature and hunting and drawing birds. He also courted the daughter of one of his neighbors, Lucy Bakewell, who would become his wife in 1808. Unfortunately, only one of the bird sketches from Audubon's first stay in America survives.

The earliest group of extant drawings was made in Nantes, to which Audubon returned for a year-long stay with his family in 1805. Inscribed "Près Nantes" at the lower right, Audubon's pencil and pastel drawing *Avocet* describes this large shore bird with simple elegance and a sharp eye for detail (opposite). The artist has interrupted the bird's profile in order to display its strong, webbed feet from the front. A clear, graceful curve renders the upturned beak that the Avocet uses to secure food by swinging it side to side through soft, wet ground as it moves forward on its slender legs. Audubon's earliest drawing of a mammal, the

Marmot (Groundhog or Woodchuck) of 1805, is also drawn in profile, a format that Audubon would later dismiss as the "mere profile-like cut figures" of conventional natural history painting (p. 12, top). He would depart from that format by "adopting a different course of representation" to achieve a more naturalistic effect.[3] Although some mammals appear as prey in Audubon's *The Birds of America*, it was not until 1841 that he began to draw a series of animals for his last publication, *The Viviparous Quadrupeds of North America*. The *Owl*, which Audubon identified as a Large Horned or Eagle Owl in his inscription, is a rare instance among these early drawings of presenting the subject from the front (p. 12, bottom).

Accompanied by a business partner Ferdinand Rozier, Audubon returned to Pennsylvania from France in the spring of 1806 to try to sell the Mill Grove property. Drawings made in his spare time, such as the *Robin* and the *Wood Thrush*, indicate that Audubon continued to work with the profile format but began to experiment with new kinds of supports for the birds and to expand his range of color (pp. 27 and 13). He shows a Wood Thrush perched on the limb of a wild cherry; the detailed rendering of numerous cherries almost obscures the gentle contours of the thrush, a bird Audubon favored for its melodic song. A more successful marriage of bird with botanical specimen appears in Audubon's *Pine Warbler* painted in 1812. The small songbird, shot on a return visit to Mill Grove, is perched on a leaf of spiderwort at the center of the drawing. The precise details of the petite bird's markings are recorded with straightforward accuracy in pencil and pastel. Watercolor, instead, was used to describe the glorious looped-over leaves of the spiderwort. Subtle shading and adjustments in contour give thickness, weight, and motion to the stem and leaves of the plant. The thin parallel lines of leaf veining create a pattern that responds to the bend of the leaves. The pattern disappears in shadow and becomes sharply focused by light. The design and rendering of the spiderwort has the vivacity and abstract elegance of Oriental calligraphy. The beauty of this botanical drawing, which may have been added later to the composition by Audubon's assistant Joseph Mason, reflects Audubon's belief that a true lover of nature admires and studies all facets of the natural world. "Every individual, possessed of a sound heart, listens with delight to the love notes of the woodland warblers," he wrote. "He never casts a glance upon their lovely forms without proposing to himself questions respecting them; nor does he look on the trees which they frequent, or the flowers over which they glide, without admiring their grandeur, or delighting in their sweet odours or their brilliant tints."[4]

The most dramatic composition from this period is the *Osprey*, in which the hawk, with its bill opened wide, bends its head toward the fish prey grasped firmly in its talons (p. 17). This lively posture may be the first produced by a new technique and apparatus invented by Audubon. As he described it, "my drawings have all been made after individuals fresh killed, mostly by myself, and put up before me by means of wires, & c. in the precise attitude presented, and copied with a closeness of measurement that I hope will always correspond with nature when brought into contact."[5] A model of such a wired armature with specimens of Blue Jays was prepared in 1984 at the American Museum of Natural History

Avocet

Audubon's name: Avoset. 1805.
Pencil and pastel on paper, 18⅜ × 12″.
By permission of the Houghton Library, Harvard University.

This work, one of Audubon's earliest existing drawings, was made in 1805, in Nantes, France. Audubon spent a year in France visiting his parents at their house near the Loire River. In 1806, upon his return to the United States, he gave the bird drawings that he had made while he was away to Lucy Bakewell, who became his wife in 1808. Typical of his work at this time, this drawing of an Avocet is done in pencil and pastel and shows the bird in stiff profile.

In 1814, Audubon spotted Avocets in a pond in Indiana and he wondered why they were so far from the sea. After studying them at a distance for a few days, he crept through knee-deep mud to their island nesting place in the middle of the pond. "Softly, and on all fours, I crawled toward the spot, panting with heat and anxiety. Now, Reader, I am actually within three feet of the unheeding creature, peeping at her through the tall grasses. Lovely bird! How innocent, how unsuspecting, and yet how near to thine enemy, albeit he be an admirer of thy race! There she sits on her eggs, her head almost mournfully sunk among the plumage, and her eyes, unanimated by the sight of her mate, half-closed, as if she dreamed of future scenes." (Ornithological Biography, 4:4, 170)

Marmot

1805. Pencil and pastel on paper, 20¼ × 26¼".
By permission of the Houghton Library, Harvard
University.

*Dated June 6, 1805, this may be one of
Audubon's earliest studies of a mammal,
and it demonstrates his early insistence
upon precise detail. Each hair on the marmot's coat and each whisker on his nose is
described with a careful stroke. Two feces
pellets are included under the tail.*

*Animals were depicted as prey in some
of Audubon's bird paintings, but he did
not begin to make animals the central subject of his drawings until 1841. In 1843
during his Missouri River trip, he was
able to observe marmots on numerous
occasions. "Marmots are quite abundant," he noted in his journal during the
trip, "and here they perforate their holes in
the loose, sandy soil of the river banks, as
well as the same soil wherever it is somewhat elevated." (*Journals, *1:458)*

Owl

1805. Pencil and pastel on paper, 26 × 20".
By permission of the Houghton Library, Harvard
University.

*Audubon made this pencil and pastel
drawing in Nantes, France, in 1805. The
artist's inscription identifies it as a Large
Horned or Eagle Owl.*

*Calling these birds "the Nimrods" of the
woods, Audubon observed that "the flight
of the Great Horned Owl is elevated, rapid
and graceful. Now and then it glides
silently close over the earth, with incompa-
rable velocity, and drops, as if shot dead,
on the prey beneath. At other times, it suddenly alights on the top of a fence-stake or
a dead stump, shakes its feathers,
arranges them, and utters a shriek so hor-
rid that the woods around echo to its
dismal sound." (*Ornithological Biography, *1:313, 314) This active, noisy
bird appears somewhat stiff and still in
this rendering that is typical of Audubon's
early work.*

Wood Thrush

Audubon's name: Wood Thrush. 1806.
Watercolor and graphite on paper, 15¾ × 9¾″.
By permission of the Houghton Library, Harvard
University.

"This bird is my greatest favourite of the feathered tribes of our woods," Audubon declared of the Wood Thrush, pictured in an early drawing perched on a wild cherry branch. *"To it I owe much. How often has it revived my drooping spirits, when I have listened to its wild notes in the forest, after passing a restless night in my slender shed."* (Ornithological Biography, 1:372) Audubon seldom mentioned the Wood Thrush without praising its flute-like song, *"always sweet and mellow,"* and he often felt homesick longing for it while away in Europe. *"Never before did I so long for a glimpse of our rich magnolia woods,"* he wrote from Edinburgh. *"I never before felt the want of a glance at our forests as I do now; could I be there but a moment, hear the mellow Mock-bird, or the Wood-thrush, to me always so pleasing, how happy should I be."* (Journals, 2:316)

PLATE XXX.

Pine Warbler

Audubon's name: Vigors's Vireo. 1812. Robert
Havell, engraver.
Hand-colored etching and aquatint, 19½ × 12¼".
New York Public Library.

*Audubon shot the Pine Warbler that
served as the model for his drawing while
revisiting Mill Grove, his father's former
estate near Valley Forge, in 1812. Years
later, believing he had discovered a new
species, he named it Vigors's Vireo, after
the English naturalist, Nicholas A. Vigors. The Pine Warbler, which is found in
the open pine woods and barrens of eastern North America, is shown perched on a
frond of spiderwort, which may have been
painted by Audubon's assistant, Joseph
Mason.*

*"I am unable to give any account of the
habits of a species which I have honoured
with the name of a naturalist whose merits are so well known to the learned
world," Audubon recorded regretfully.
"The individual represented in the plate, I
shot upwards of twenty years ago, and
have never met with another of its kind. It
was in the month of May, on a small
island of the Perkioming Creek, forming
part of my farm of Mill Grove."*
(Ornithological Biography, *1:153*)

Vigors's Warbler
SYLVIA VIGORSII, *Aud.*
Male. —
Virginian Spiderwort. Tradescantia virginica.

Drawn from Nature and Published by John J. Audubon, F.R.S. F.L.S.

Engraved, Printed & Coloured by R. Havell.

Blackburnian Warbler.

SYLVIA BLACKBURNIA. Leth.

Male.

Phlox maculata.

Drawn from Nature by J.J.Audubon F.R.S. F.L.S.

Engraved, Printed & Coloured by R.Havell,London,1832.

Blackburnian Warbler

Audubon's name: Blackburnian Warbler. 1812.
Robert Havell, engraver.
Hand-colored etching and aquatint, 19⅝ × 12¼″.
New York Public Library.

An early drawing of the Blackburnian Warbler made on May 12, 1812, from a specimen "procured near Reading in Pennsylvania, on the banks of the Schuykill River" served as the model for the engraving by Robert Havell, Jr. (Ornithological Biography, 2:209) *With the affection of an old friend and admirer, Audubon later wrote about sighting the warbler in a far more remote location. "On the Magdalene Islands, in the Gulf of St. Lawrence, which I visited in June 1833, I found the Blackburnian Warbler in all the brilliancy of its spring plumage, and had the pleasure of hearing its sweet song, while it was engaged in pursuing its insect prey among the branches of a fir tree, moving along somewhat in the manner of the American Redstart. Its song, which consisted of five or six notes, was so much louder than could have been expected from the size of the bird, that it was not until I had fairly caught it in the act, that I felt satisfied as to its proceeding from my old acquaintance."* (Ornithological Biography, 2:208)

Red-winged Blackbird

Audubon's name: Red-winged Starling or Marsh Blackbird. 1810.
Pencil and pastel on paper, 14¾ × 8½".
By permission of the Houghton Library, Harvard University.

This animated pastel, drawn in 1810 in Henderson, Kentucky, depicts the male Red-winged Blackbird on a branch of milkweed. This gregarious blackbird, which travels and congregates in large flocks, is present throughout North America, breeding in swamps, marshes, and hayfields. With a diet that includes small fruits, seeds, and grain, the bird's "pilferings," Audubon suggested, "might induce the young student of nature to conceive that it had been created for the purpose of annoying the farmer." (Ornithological Biography, *1:348*)

Describing the migrations of the Red-winged Blackbird, Audubon wrote, "They frequently alight on trees of moderate size, spread their tail, swell out their plummage [sic], and utter their clear and not unmusical notes, particularly in the early morning, before their departure from the neighborhood of the places in which they have roosted; for their migrations, you must know, are performed entirely during the day." (Ornithological Biography, *1:348*) *Additional observations made in Galveston led Audubon to the general hypothesis "that migration in birds is far from being regular, but is dependent on many accidental circumstances, such as difference of temperature at certain seasons when they are supposed usually to move, or storms, or want of proper food."* (Ornithological Biography, *5:488*)

drawn from Nature by J.J. Audubon

Fish Hawk or Osprey A. Wilson
Faucon Pecheur de la Caroline de Buffon
Falco Haliaetus

Osprey

Audubon's name: Fish Hawk. 1806.
Pencil, pastel, and watercolor on paper,
20⅝ × 24⅞".
By permission of the Houghton Library, Harvard
University.

"The motions of the Fish Hawk in the air are graceful, and as majestic as those of the Eagle," Audubon wrote. "It rises with ease to a great height by extensive circlings performed apparently by mere inclinations of the wings and tail. It dives at times to some distance with the wings partially closed, and resumes its sailing, as if these plunges were made for amusement only." (Ornithological Biography, 1:416) Audubon's technique—which he invented —of wiring freshly killed birds in natural positions accounts for the lifelike quality of this early drawing, made at Mill Grove, his father's estate, in 1806. The Osprey is drawn in pastel, with watercolor highlighting the bill and eye.

Audubon's notes on the Osprey reveal his determination to see nature fresh and to trust his own observations almost exclusively. "I have frequently heard it asserted," he remarked, "that the Fish Hawk is sometimes drawn under water and drowned, when it has attempted to seize a fish which is too strong for it, and that some of these birds have been found sticking by their talons to the back of Sturgeons and other large fishes. But, as nothing of this kind ever came under my observation, I am unable to corroborate these reports." (Ornithological Biography, 1:420)

(opposite). This apparatus allowed Audubon to work rapidly in the field by immediately setting his bird specimen into the active posture that would appear in the finished work. Simultaneously he could quickly record the vibrant colors of a "freshly killed" bird before they faded. Since he noted that the eye and bill of the shot bird lost their natural colors most rapidly, he used watercolor for those parts of the Osprey to capture their lifelike tints.

Although Audubon spent much of his leisure time in the United States seeking birds and perfecting his style of painting them, his primary goal was to make his fortune in business. In 1807, Audubon and Rozier opened a general store in Louisville, Kentucky, to capitalize on the growing trade of this Ohio River town. The following year Audubon brought his new bride Lucy to Louisville, a place they both would cherish for its beautiful site on the riverbank, its abundant fish and game, "but, above all, the generous hospitality of the inhabitants, and the urbanity of their manners."[6] Rozier and Audubon moved their business from Louisville to the small town of Henderson, Kentucky, where in 1819 after a series of partnership changes it ultimately failed. "I could not bear to give the attention required by my business," Audubon wrote wryly, later on, "and, therefore my business abandoned me."[7] In spite of the commercial difficulties and the attendant personal hardships that characterized the Audubons' life in Kentucky, where both their sons—Victor Gifford (born 1809) and John Woodhouse (born 1812)—were raised, the family resided there longer than anywhere else in their lives, and always remembered it fondly as their home.

It was in Kentucky in 1809 that Audubon painted the Cooper's Hawk in the lower right corner of his painting of three birds combined into one composition entitled *Northern Goshawk and Cooper's Hawk* (p. 25). The Cooper's Hawk typifies Audubon's early bird drawings in its upright, immobile posture taken from the profile view. The artist used pastel with graphite highlights to describe the color and field markings of the bird, and to indicate some differentiations in texture, he applied watercolor to the bill and eye. He painted the adult Northern Goshawk, pictured at lower left, a few years later (1810–1819) in much the same way. Audubon was pleased enough with these early profile portraits to save them and later cut them out and and include them as collage additions to a drawing of an immature Northern Goshawk painted around 1829. This intriguing drawing allows us to trace on one sheet some of the principal stylistic and methodological developments in Audubon's art during these formative years. The young Northern Goshawk, positioned at the top, grips the branch support with its talons, opens its bill, and spreads its wings in an active, horizontal pose. Although he adopted a largely profile view of the bird, Audubon subtly twisted its body by spreading the legs along the branch and unfolding its wings. This reveals additional breast and wing feathers, suggesting a three-dimensional being moving through space.

When the artist combined these three separate drawings onto a single sheet, he made no attempt to relate the birds to each other in any thematic way. He showed them as independent specimens of three separate species of hawk, as he believed them to be. Nor did Audubon provide a setting to unite the birds into a

Wired Model of Blue Jays

Prepared by David Schwendeman for the American Museum of Natural History. Courtesy, Department of Library Services, American Museum of Natural History, New York.

This wired model of blue jays recreates Audubon's technical invention for posing birds for his original watercolors. The recently shot specimens could be quickly mounted into life-like positions for the artist to study and represent before the colors of the dead birds began to fade.

David Schwendeman, the taxidermist at the American Museum of Natural History, re-created an example of Audubon's invention for an exhibit, "Science into Art." The blue jays were not gathered by Audubon. He disposed of his specimens immediately after use and did not preserve the skins. However, at the time of his death, Audubon owned a collection of several hundred bird skins, almost entirely, if not entirely, prepared by others.

Bonaparte's Gull

Audubon's name: Bonapartian Gull. 1821 and 1830. Watercolor and collage on paper, 21⅜₁₆ × 15⅜₁₆".
Collection of The New-York Historical Society.

Audubon first observed and obtained specimens of these gulls in 1819 in Cincinnati. It was on an outing with Robert Best, then curator of the Cincinnati Museum, where Audubon worked, providing painted backgrounds for the natural history exhibits. The two men watched "two Gulls sweeping gracefully over the tranquil waters [of the Ohio River]. Now they would alight side by side, as if intent on holding a close conversation . . . We watched them for nearly half an hour, and having learned something of their manners, shot one, which happened to be a female. On her dropping, her mate almost immediately alighted beside her, and was shot," Audubon reported in a matter-of-fact manner. Waxing poetic, Audubon concluded that "there, side by side, as in life, so in death, floated the lovely birds." (Ornithological Biography, 4:212)

In this watercolor drawing, Audubon shows two mature gulls, a black-headed male and a brown-headed female, with a young gull in the foreground. All three birds were painted on separate sheets and then glued onto a single sheet to form this stylized composition. In the engraving the stark, almost abstract, design of the original watercolor drawing of the birds is enclosed in a landscape context, including a sandy shore with white cliffs in the distance across the water.

PLATE LXXV.

Le Petit Caporal.
FALCO TEMERARIUS.
Male.

Merlin

Audubon's name: Pigeon Hawk or Le Petit Caporal.
1812. Robert Havell, engraver.
Hand-colored etching and aquatint, 19½ × 12¼″.
New York Public Library.

When Audubon drew this bird, on April 23, 1812, in Pennsylvania, he thought he had discovered a new species and named it Le Petit Caporal, or Falco temerarius, after Napoleon Bonaparte's nickname among his troops. Writing in his Ornithological Biography *years later, however, he recognized that "the bird represented . . . and described under the name of Falco temerarius, was merely a beautiful adult of the Pigeon Hawk, F. columbarius." (*Ornithological Biography, 5:368*) The Pigeon Hawk is now known as a Merlin, a kind of falcon.*

*Audubon referred to the Pigeon Hawk, or Merlin, as "the little marauder" and "the little plunderer" for its swift, efficient, and usually successful seizures of other birds, such the Red-breasted Thrush and the Wild Pigeon. (*Ornithological Biography, 1:467*) To Audubon's amusement, however, the Merlin was once thwarted by its intended prey while Audubon watched. "We saw a Pigeon Hawk giving chase to a Spotted Sandpiper on the wing," he related. "When the hawk was about to seize the little fellow it dove under water and escaped. This was repeated five or six times; to my great surprise and pleasure, the Hawk was obliged to relinquish the prey." (*Journals, 2:162*)

Broad-winged Hawk

Audubon's name: Broad-winged Hawk. 1829.
Robert Havell, engraver.
Hand-colored etching and aquatint, 37¾ × 25¼″.
New York Public Library.

The Broad-winged Hawk is small and chunky, with distinctive black and white tail-banding, and has a range that reaches from southern Canada through the eastern United States down to the Gulf states. Audubon captured a female hawk from its nest on May 27, 1812, at Fatland Ford Plantation, near Valley Forge, Pennsylvania. He recounted the unusual circumstances that allowed him to draw a live and unrestrained bird in his room. "I put the bird on a stick made fast to my table. It merely moved its feet to grasp the stick, and stood erect, but raised its feathers, and drew in its neck on its shoulders. I passed my hand over it, to smooth the feathers by gentle pressure. It moved not. The plumage remained as I wished it. Its eye, directed towards mine, appeared truly sorrowful, with a degree of pensiveness, which rendered me at that moment quite uneasy. I measured the length of its bill with the compass, began my outlines, continued measuring part after part as I went on, and finished the drawing, without the bird ever moving once." (Ornithological Biography, 1:461–462) After making the drawing, Audubon set the hawk free out his window. The drawing of this pair was completed only in 1829, when Audubon procured a male specimen to complement the female. The painting of the pignut branch was provided by George Lehman, a Swiss-German artist from Pennsylvania, who assisted with the backgrounds of some of Audubon's works at this time.

single spatial context. When the engraver, Robert Havell, added a landscape of a riverbank with a mountain in the distance to his engraving of this image, the three birds maintained a surreal isolation from each other and from their setting (p. 24). A similarly composed image can be found in Audubon's watercolor drawing of Bonaparte's Gull (p. 20). All three birds were drawn separately and later brought together on one sheet, without the artist's adapting their scale to one another or to their setting. This additive approach to composition lends the work an abstract flatness of design, with the background negative shapes asserting themselves as positive forms in a way that is appealing to the modern eye.

Devastating events in the life of the Audubon family took place in 1819 and precipitated abrupt changes in the artist's personal and professional directions. The Audubons' daughter, Lucy, had died in 1817 at the age of two; in 1819 a second daughter, Rose, was born and died seven months later. The failure of his business venture in Henderson, Kentucky, that same year caused Audubon to go to prison for unpaid debts and to declare bankruptcy. On his release from prison, faced with a desperate personal and financial situation, Audubon left Kentucky and moved to Cincinnati, Ohio, in 1820 to take a job as a taxidermist at the newly established Western Museum of Cincinnati College. Although his stay in Cincinnati was short, it was there that he decided to make a profession of his passion for hunting and drawing birds.

Audubon was hired for the museum position by Dr. Daniel Drake, a founder of the Western Museum Society and a kind of Renaissance man, who was exactly the same age as Audubon. Physician, druggist, businessman, philanthropist, civic leader, and editor, Drake was known as "the Franklin of the Ohio Valley." Although Audubon only stayed at the museum a few months, Drake offered him the first opportunity to transform his avocation into a vocation. With Robert Best, the museum's curator, he gathered specimens of birds and fish, learned more about how to stuff them, and prepared habitat scenery for their display. The salary for this ideal job, however, was neither dependable nor sufficient to support Audubon and his family. Lucy took in private pupils and Audubon turned to teaching art and making portraits of Cincinnati residents to supplement his income. "To be a good draughtsman in those days was to me a blessing," wrote Audubon. "I at once undertook to take portraits of the human head Divine in black chalk, and thanks to my master, David, succeeded admirably. I commenced at exceeding low prices, but raised these prices as I became more known in this capacity."[8]

Despite numerous efforts by scholars and biographers to substantiate it, Audubon's claim that he had studied art with the renowned French neoclassical painter Jacques-Louis David (1748–1825) is probably false.[9] This invention of art training at the prestigious French academy in Paris, which Audubon's writing mentions more than once, helped form his elevated artistic identity. Audubon wanted to present himself in the New World as an artist with a European pedigree, and not just as an ambitious entrepreneur. He undoubtedly felt that the imprimatur of academic schooling would win the admiration and respect of his culturally insecure American audience. It is possible that, through repetition,

Northern Goshawk

Audubon's name: Goshawk. *Cooper's Hawk.*
Audubon's name: Stanley Hawk. 1809 and c. 1829.
Robert Havell, engraver. Hand-colored etching and
aquatint, 38½ × 25¼".
New York Public Library.

The stilted character of the composition in the aquatint engraving of Northern Goshawks and Cooper's Hawk derives from Audubon's use of collage in the original drawing. The birds were cut from separate drawings and pasted together on a single sheet. The artist did not pencil in instructions for a landscape background, leaving the engraver, Robert Havell, to complete the scene with a grass marsh and, in the distance, a mountain.

Northern Goshawk

Audubon's name: Goshawk. *Cooper's Hawk.*
Audubon's name: Stanley Hawk. Cooper's Hawk
painted on Dec. 5, 1809 in Louisville, KY; adult
Northern Goshawk painted between 1810 and
1819 in Henderson, KY; immature goshawk painted
c. 1829.
Watercolor, pastel, graphite, gouache, selective
glazing, and collage on paper, 39 × 25⅞".
Collection of The New-York Historical Society.

This work combines two early pastel drawings pasted on a sheet below a later, more mature watercolor, and offers an overview of Audubon's development as an artist, The Cooper's Hawk, at lower right, was painted in 1809, and the Northern Goshawk, at lower left, was painted between 1810 and 1819. The stiffness of their poses contrasts with the lovely depiction of the immature goshawk, at top, which Audubon painted c. 1829. Years after making his early drawings, and before the engraving of these images, Audubon described the rigidity of his early style. "On the 5th of December 1809, I made a drawing of the male of this species [Cooper's Hawk], in its matured state of of colouring, at Louisville, in Kentucky, where I then resided. That drawing is now before me, and the bird which it represents is to this day undescribed. The figure would have been engraved, had it not been as stiff, and as little indicative of life, as those usually seen in books on Natural History." (Ornithological Biography, 1:187)

These birds are both accipiters, hawks with long tails and short wings. They prey chiefly on birds and also on small mammals in the woodlands where they reside. The Cooper's Hawk and the Northern Goshawk are both widespread but uncommon in America.

Mr. Thomas Best and *Mrs. Thomas Best*

1820. Black chalk, background possibly touched with neutral wash, 11¾ × 10″ and 11⅜ × 9⅝″. M. and M. Karolik Collection. Courtesy, Museum of Fine Arts, Boston.

Audubon taught himself to paint portraits for practical reasons. In 1820, after moving to Cincinnati with his family, he painted the residents there to supplement his income. He could command five dollars apiece, and because of his facility in the genre he became popular and successful. The drawings of Mr. and Mrs. Thomas Best, residents of Cincinnati, were typical of Audubon's work in their bust-length format and the use of pencil and charcoal (or black chalk). Audubon left Cincinnati within a year, but continued drawing portraits, at intervals, until 1826.

this mythical background began to acquire a measure of reality for the artist himself. At least, it may have steeled the backbone of his self-esteem to meet the financial and personal challenges that beset his developing years as an artist.

Audubon's pencil and charcoal portraits of *Thomas Best* and *Mrs. Thomas Best* of Cincinnati, made in the summer of 1820, are characteristic of the artist's work in this genre. His sure control of linear contour and subtle modeling of light and shade were coupled with the precise renderings of individual characteristics. With his sharp eye, he noticed an angled brow, a narrow upper lip, and a hooded eyelid, and he traced them carefully to create recognizable likenesses of his sitters. This developing ability to particularize, in the more than one hundred portraits that Audubon made between 1819 and 1826, paralleled, and perhaps contributed to, a similar development in his bird drawings during the same years.

Dr. Drake offered Audubon the opportunity of exhibiting a selection of his bird drawings at the Western Museum. An article by Benjamin Powers (brother of the sculptor Hiram Powers) in the *Cincinnati Inquisitor Advertiser*, published in February 1820, gave notice of Audubon's arrival in the city and of his intention to teach the art of drawing. It encouraged the citizens of Cincinnati to take advantage of the current museum display of the artist's collection of bird drawings. "No one can examine them without the strongest emotions of surprise and admiration," Powers asserted. "We hope every person who feels an interest in the subject will avail himself of the first opportunity to examine specimens in this branch of the fine arts, which, for fidelity and correctness in the execution, are so excellent as to surpass, in our judgment, all others that we have ever witnessed."[10]

The professional respect and critical approbation of his work as a naturalist that Audubon enjoyed in Cincinnati gave him the confidence to put his commercial failures behind him and turn his attention to nature. Sometime during his seven-month stay in that city, he formulated the idea of developing for publication a complete set of drawings of all the birds in the United States.

To embark on this ambitious project, the artist enlisted the help of a thirteen-year-old student in his drawing class named Joseph Mason (1808–1842) and set off on a simple flatboat down the Ohio and Mississippi Rivers with the destination of New Orleans. With the support of the small nest egg from portrait drawings, he left his wife and sons behind to attempt a project that only just recently had been accomplished. Audubon had cited in his own hand on a number of his early drawings, such as the *Wood Thrush* and the *Robin* (pp. 13 and 27), the name "A. Wilson," as the source for the identification of the bird. This referred to Alexander Wilson (1766–1813; see p. 28), the Scottish artist and poet whose nine-volume work *American Ornithology* (1808–1813) was the first comprehensive publication devoted to the description and illustration of American birds (pp. 29, 58 and 99). And it was well known to Audubon, who had met Wilson in Louisville, Kentucky, in 1810, when the older ornithologist showed Audubon sample colored plates and asked him to subscribe to the work.

La Litorne du Canada Måle
New york, January 4.ᵗʰ 1807.
J.J.A.
Nº 102

Robin A. Wilson
Turdus Migratorius
Litorne du Canada Buffon —
drawn by J. J. Audubon Jany. 4. 1807 — New York

Eggs 4 — 5.ᵗʰ May
Lonely Bay —

American Robin

Audubon's name: American Robin or Migratory Thrush. 1807. Pencil, pastel, and watercolor on paper, 9½ × 13½".
By permission of the Houghton Library.

This early drawing was made in January 1807 in New York City, where Audubon spent the winter as a clerk in the import and export business of Benjamin Bakewell, his future uncle-in-law. It is the first of Audubon's three drawings of American Robins, a comparison of which shows the artist's stylistic development over two decades (see p. 64). The American Robin, or Migratory Thrush, as Audubon also called it, remained a favorite of his, especially on his journeys far from home. "The first land-bird seen by me when I stepped upon the rugged shores of Labrador, was the Robin," Audubon wrote. *"Its joyful notes were the first that saluted my ear. . . . The absence of trees, . . . the barren aspect of all around, the sombre mantle of the mountainous distance that hung along the horizon, excited the most melancholy feelings; and I could scarcely refrain from shedding tears when I heard the song of the Thrush, sent there as if to reconcile me to my situation."* (Ornithological Biography, 2:190)

Rembrandt Peale. *Portrait of Alexander Wilson*

c. 1809–13. Oil on canvas, 20¼ × 16¹¹⁄₁₆″.
American Philosophical Society, Philadelphia.

In 1810, while living in Louisville, Kentucky, Audubon had a meeting with Alexander Wilson (1766–1813), the Scottish poet, artist, and schoolmaster who published American Ornithology *(1808–1813), a nine-volume set of descriptions and illustrations of American birds. "How well do I remember him, as he walked up to me!" Audubon later wrote. "His long, rather hooked nose, the keenness of his eyes, and his prominent cheek bones, stamped his countenance with a peculiar character." (Journals, 2:200–201) Unlike Audubon, Wilson enjoyed the support of the Philadelphia scientific community, especially Charles Willson Peale (1741–1827), whose son Rembrandt (1778–1860) painted this portrait.*

Audubon later recalled that he almost subscribed to the publication, but stopped when his partner Rozier told him that, at $120, the subscription was too expensive and that his own bird drawings were of superior quality anyway. Audubon remembered loaning Wilson some of his own drawings of birds that were new to the Scotsman and hosting Wilson on a birding tour of Louisville. Wilson's diary made little mention of Audubon's hospitality, and the different impressions of this encounter fueled an angry debate some years later between advocates of Wilson's work and Audubon's supporters.

The more important consequence of Audubon's acquaintance with Alexander Wilson's project was that it introduced him to the possibility of documenting and drawing birds as a professional undertaking rather than as a pastime. Later, when he conceived of a publication of his own, Wilson's *American Ornithology* set a standard against which to compete. Indeed, just one day out, on his first river trip to gather specimens and make drawings for *The Birds of America*, Audubon noted an error in Wilson's findings. A bird that Wilson had identified as a separate species of warbler and called an Autumnal Warbler, Audubon asserted was, instead, not a distinct species but an immature Yellow-rumped Warbler. "This was a Young Male in beautiful plumage for the season and I Drew it—as I feel perfectly Convinced that Mr. Willson has made an Error in presenting this Bird as a New Specie."[11]

On the first day of that voyage, October 12, 1820, the most impressive characteristic of Audubon's journal record is the clear expression of his confidence. Setting out with his teenaged companion, Joseph Mason, Audubon declared that he "left Cincinnati this afternoon at half past 4 o'clock, on Board of Mr. Jacob Aumack's flat Boat—bound to New Orleans—the feeling of a Husband and a Father, were My Lot when I kissed My Beloved Wife & Children with an expectation of being absent for Seven Months." Acknowledging that he had no money to fall back on, he nevertheless embarked with a "determined mind" to fulfill his goal of finding, drawing, and publishing all the birds of the United States with unprecedented accuracy and completeness. "My Talents are to be My Support and My enthusiasm my Guide in My Difficulties, the whole of which I am ready to exert to meet, and to surmount," asserted Audubon.[12]

In the company of the other passengers—two Pennsylvania carpenters, an uncouth, womanizing jokester, and a Bostonian who owned the cargo—plus a couple of rough crew members, Audubon and Mason spent three months on this cargo boat before reaching New Orleans. He took advantage of the ark's slow pace to take a skiff out ahead on the river or to go hunting ashore, seeking, observing, and shooting birds. He measured them, weighed them, examined their eggs (p. 30), and opened their stomachs to record the food that they ate. He made drawings of them and he noted down many of his observations in his faltering English, with its tentative grasp of spelling and grammar. "About Two hours before sun sett a *Barred Owl* teased by four Crows and Chased from the tree where he was Lit raised up in the manner of a Hawk in the air so high that We Lost Entire sight of him, he acted as if Lost—now & then making very short Circles and flapping his Wings quickly, then zig zag lines—this was quite a new Sight

Drawn from Nature by Titian R. Peale.

Engraved by W.H. Lizars.

Wild Turkey. Male & Female.
Meleagris Gallopavo.

9.

Titian Peale (1800–1885).
Wild Turkey, Male and Female

W. H. Lizars, engraver.
Hand-colored etching, 8 ¾ x 5½″.
From the 1832 edition of Alexander Wilson's *American Ornithology. . .*, edited by Sir William Jardine and incorporating Charles Lucien Bonaparte's continuation of Wilson's work. Vol. 3, Plate 9.
New Yorkublic Library.

Wilson's editor, Sir William Jardine, wrote: "We have particular satisfaction in acknowledging the kindness of Mr. John J. Audubon, from whom we have received a copious narrative, containing a considerable portion of the valuable notes collected by him, on this bird [the Wild Turkey]. His observations, principally made in Kentucky and Louisiana, proved the more interesting, as we have received no information from those states; we have, in consequence, been enabled to enrich the present article with several new details of the manners and habits of the wild turkey." (American Ornithology; or The Natural History of the Birds of the United States, *3 vols. Edited by Sir William Jardine. London: Whittaker, Treacher & Arnot, 1832).*

Six Eggs

1821. Pencil and watercolor on paper, 8¼ × 11″.
Collection, Louisiana State Museum, New Orleans.

Although Audubon featured eggs only rarely in his drawings, he frequently included them in his detailed descriptions of birds and their characteristics. Here the artist has depicted the eggs of six different birds, which he labeled Orchard Oriole, Carolina Pigeon, Mockingbird, Wild Turkey, Bluebird, and Carolina Wren. Each egg is labeled, with the number of eggs usually laid by each species indicated beneath it. Additional notes beside the egg of the Carolina Wren detail possible variations in the eggs of that bird.

and I expect takes place but seldom—I felt anxious to see his Descent to the Earth but could not—" he wrote, on Wednesday, November 8, 1820, capturing his breathless wonder at an unusual performance in flight.[13] This is but one of many occasions during the course of Audubon's lifetime that he would have the opportunity of observing the habits of the Barred Owl. However, the vividness of this first impression no doubt contributed to the liveliness of the watercolor drawing of this elegantly patterned bird. The *Barred Owl* is shown with wings spread and engaged in some manner with an unseen companion or combatant (p. 34). The mystery is solved in the engraving after this drawing, which includes an Eastern gray squirrel that Audubon had figured on a separate sheet (p. 36) and asked Robert Havell to include on the same plate (p. 35).

In the same journal, Audubon made an early observation of some Native Americans that he spotted in a canoe. The "sons of nature," as he called them, fascinated the artist, and he made notes about the appearances, habits, and lifestyles of the many different tribes he encountered during the course of his travels. At the junction of the Ohio and Mississippi Rivers, Audubon observed "two Indians in a Canoe. They spoke some French, had bear traps, uncommonly clean kept, a few Venaison (*sic*) hams, a gun, and Looked so Independent, free & unconcerned with the World that I Gazed on them, admired their Spirits, & wished for their condition."[14] Audubon's longing for the unencumbered life of the Indians he witnessed was not a purely personal view. It was shared by many Europeans who regarded the Native American as the embodiment of their own dream of returning to an uncorrupted, natural state. They conceived of Indians as "noble savages," content in an innocent harmony with nature and uncontaminated by the constructs of civilization. For Europeans, the Native American, like the continent itself, took on the dimension of a paradisiacal fantasy. He was perceived as a kind of original man in a perfect condition of moral and physical grace. Audubon would have had to go no further than to the works of his own countryman, the eighteenth-century French Romantic writer Jean-Jacques Rousseau (1712–1778), to be informed of this idealized view. In his *Discourse on the Origins of Inequality*, Rousseau describes the development of man from a happy, self-sufficient brute to an unhappy victim of civilization. A Romantic hero, like Emile, in Rousseau's novel of the same name, educated in a state of natural freedom, responding only to the requirements of self-preservation and the demands of his own senses, exemplified this human ideal. Emile could have provided a partial role model for Audubon's own fictional persona as a man formed by his interaction with nature.

In later years, impressions of Native Americans that Audubon recorded in his journals reflected another view of these people that also had its roots in European culture, for Europeans saw Native Americans as embodiments of their fears as well as their dreams. In this alternative view, Native Americans were motivated by base human passion and uncontrolled by law and religion, and thus took on subhuman proportions in the convictions of the Europeans who exploited this view to bolster their racial, moral, and economic superiority. On his Missouri trip in 1843, Audubon and his fellow travelers frequently traded and bartered with

Indians. At Fort Union, Audubon witnessed a group of Indians yelling and singing wildly as they approached. "They all looked miserably poor," he wrote, and "filthy beyond description, and their black faces and foully smelling Buffalo robes made them appear to me like so many devils."[15] He complained more than once at having to shake the hands of these "dirty wretches," and he deemed a few Indians squaws "of the lowest grade of morality."[16] His impressions of some of the Indian tribes he met differed from those of the artist George Catlin (1796–1872). He doubted the truth of Catlin's paintings and descriptions of Indian life on several occasions. These challenges to the reliability of an authority reflect, in some measure, Audubon's strong competitive spirit. He challenged the findings of Alexander Wilson often for the same reason.

From 1832–1840, Catlin traveled extensively in the United States, visited almost fifty different tribes and made over five hundred oil sketches of the people and their customs and dress. The artist formed an "Indian Gallery" from these works, which was exhibited at Clinton Hall in New York City in 1837 and subsequently in Boston, Philadelphia, Washington, and London (p. 33). He published his findings in the two-volume 1841 book entitled *Illustrations of the Manners, Customs, and Condition of the North American Indian with Letters and Notes Written During Eight Years of Travel and Adventure Among the Wildest and Most Remarkable Tribes Now Existing*. Audubon called Catlin's publication "altogether humbug" when he met some members of the Assiniboine nation himself. Describing them as "very dirty," Audubon remarked that "when and where Mr. [George] Catlin saw these Indians as he has represented them, dressed in magnificent attire, with all sorts of extravagant accouterments, is more than I can divine."[17]

There may be reasons beyond the desire to discredit a competitor that prompted Audubon to form different impressions of certain Indian cultures. The passage by Congress of the various Indian Removal Acts displaced many eastern tribes to the west, a dislocation that devastated every ethnic group involved. Audubon also doubted Catlin's visual rendering of Mandan mud huts, calling their uniform size and shape as well as their orderly arrangement "poetical." Perhaps the decimated condition of the Mandan villages that Audubon encountered was the result of another assault suffered by the Native American community. A virulent small pox epidemic had swept through the western regions and ravaged the Missouri and Platte River tribes during the 1830s, after Catlin's drawings were made, and before Audubon arrived.

Audubon took careful notes of the weather conditions almost every day on his 1820 trip to New Orleans. On one of the many unpleasant, rainy days, feeling homesick, fearful, and alone, he commenced a short life sketch, starting with his own father's background, for his sons Victor and John. Should he not survive, it would be something for them to remember him by, as he wished to be remembered. Like some later autobiographies, it contains distortions. It was a quick portrait with some blemishes smoothed over. In this version, Audubon omits the place of his birth and suggests, perhaps partially to spare the feelings of his sons, that his father remarried in France after the death of his mother, and it was this second wife who raised him. To justify his current ambitious project to describe

George Catlin. *Rainmaking
Among the Mandans*

1837–39. Oil on canvas, 19½ × 27".
National Museum of American Art, Smithsonian
Institution, Washington, D.C.

Barred Owl

Although Audubon likened "the discordant screams of the Barred Owl" to "the affected bursts of laughter which you may have heard from some of the fashionable members of our own species," he clearly welcomed the bird's call on his frequent journeys. (Ornithological Biography 1:242) "The notes of the Barred Owl, that grave buffoon of our western woods, never fail to gladden the camper," he wrote in 1833 from Labrador, which he found to be silent and barren. (Journals 2:404) Audubon also remarked upon the owl's poor vision during the daytime, which leaves it startled by the very squirrels upon which it preys at night. "It is for this reason," he wrote, "that I have represented the Barred Owl gazing in amazement at one of the squirrels placed only a few inches from him." (Ornithological Biography 1:244) The squirrel, which Audubon drew on a separate sheet, was inserted later into the engraving of the Barred Owl, printed by Robert Havell, Jr.

all the birds of the United States, Audubon claims that he conceived the project in his youth, thereby adding the weight of long and serious contemplation to what might have appeared as a flight of fancy. "Ever since a Boy I have had an astonishing desire to see Much of the World," wrote the artist, "and particularly to Acquire a true knowledge of the Birds of North America."[18] Despite the financial and personal hardships this project imposed upon his family, who could deny him the opportunity to fulfill a dream cherished since childhood?

EARLY LIFE AND WORK

Barred Owl
STRIX NEBULOSA, Linn.
Male.

Barred Owl

Audubon's name: Barred Owl. 1821. Robert Havell, engraver.
Hand-colored etching and aquatint, 38½ × 25¼".
New York Public Library.

This engraving of the Barred Owl modeled on Audubon's 1821 watercolor drawing (p. 34) includes the figure of a squirrel, also based on an earlier drawing (p. 33), to complete the scene depicted— that of an owl with typically poor daytime vision being startled by a squirrel.

Eastern Gray Squirrel (Carolina Gray Squirrel)

1849. Lithograph, 27½ × 23".
Courtesy, Department of Library Services,
American Museum of Natural History, New York.

"The Gray Squirrel is too well known to require any description," Audubon remarks. *"It migrates in prodigious numbers, crossing large rivers by swimming with its tail extended on the water, and traverses immense tracts of country, in search of the places where food is most abundant. During these migrations, the Squirrels are destroyed in vast quantities. Their flesh is white, very delicate, and affords excellent eating, when the animals are young."* (Ornithological Biography, 1:247) Audubon encountered the Eastern Gray, or Carolina Gray, Squirrel often during his journey along the Upper Missouri River in 1843.

The posture of the squirrel at the lower left, sitting on its hind legs, is based upon the same watercolor sketch as the squirrel in the Barred Owl engraving (p. 35), indicating that Audubon and his sons made multiple uses of original paintings in produing finished prints for the Quadrupeds.

PLATE VII.

SCIURUS CAROLINENSIS. GMELIN.

CAROLINA GRAY SQUIRREL.

Audubon Memorabilia

Hat, gun, pistol, war club, pipe, tomahawk (made by Whites for trade with Native Americans), dog harness, fabric.
Courtesy, Department of Library Services, American Museum of Natural History, New York.

This selection of Audubon memorabilia is the fruit of the artist's various trips and the aquaintances that he made along the way. The dog harness was obtained in the barren Labrador landscape, where Audubon spent the summer of 1833. There he found a harsh and inhospitable land, populated with a surprising number of birds. The rest of the objects, many of which are Native American artifacts, were acquired during his trip to the upper Missouri River in April to October of 1843.

During most of his expeditions, Audubon came into regular contact with Indians. While out west, Audubon had several companions, including Alexander

Culbertson and Edwin T. Denig, who were married to Native American women. Although Audubon admired the physical skills and ferocity of the Native Americans, he also shared in the contemporary view of Indians as an uncivilized people lacking Christian virtue and moral behavior. "We remained looking at the Indians, all Assiniboins, and very dirty," Audubon wrote in his journal during his Missouri River trip. "When and where Mr. Catlin saw these Indians as he has represented them, dressed in magnificent attire, with all sorts of extravagant accoutrements, is more than I can divine." (Journals, 2:108)

II. *Producing* The Birds of America

American Redstart

Audubon's name: American Redstart. 1821. Robert
Havell, engraver.
Hand-colored etching and aquatint, 19¾ × 12¼".
New York Public Library.

*On many occasions and in far-flung loca-
tions, including Jestico Island during his
1833 trip to Labrador and in the Black
Snake Hills of Missouri in 1843, Audubon admired the American Redstart,
which he considered the most handsome
and lively of the warblers. The American
Redstart's flight patterns were particularly intriguing. "It keeps in perpetual
motion," he wrote, "opening its beautiful
tail at every movement which it makes,
then closing it, and flirting it from side to
side, just allowing the transparent beauty
of the feathers to be seen for a moment." In
this plate, Audubon pictures the male redstart engaged in one of the "ineffectual
attacks which this bird makes on wasps
while busily occupied about their own
nests. The bird approaches and snaps at
them, but in vain; for the wasp elevating
its abdomen, protrudes its sting, which
prevents its being seized." (Ornithological Biography, 1:202–203)*

*Audubon observed these skirmishes in
1821 in Louisiana, where he made the
drawing on which this engraving is
based. The wasps' nest and the tree
branch, a hop hornbeam or ironwood, was
drawn by Joseph Mason, who was
Audubon's assistant from the autumn of
1820 until the summer of 1822.*

Although in retrospect Audubon's entire youth can be seen as a preparatory phase in the naturalist's development toward the most distinguished
work of his life—the multivolume *The Birds of America*—in fact, such a teleologi-
cal interpretation of the artist's early biography diminishes the diversity of experience and the serendipitous role played by chance in shaping his early life. If his
father had not sent him to America to make his fortune or if one of his commercial undertakings had been brilliantly successful, what course would
Audubon's career have taken? Until his trip down the Mississippi River and
arrival in New Orleans in January 1821 at the age of thirty-six, a variety of possi-
bilities could be pondered. However, when Audubon docked at New Orleans at
8 A.M. that Sunday morning, the first thing he noticed was the activity of the birds
at the waterfront. "Hundreds of Fish Crows [were] hovering near the shipping
and dashing down to the Watter [*sic*] Like Gulls for food," he remarked, "utter-
ing a cry very much like the young of the Common Crow when they first Leave
the Nests."[19] From that point until the fourth and last folio of *The Birds of America*
was published in 1838, the discovery, documentation, and publication of American birds became Audubon's primary focus. It was this project that shored up his
self-confidence with single-minded dedication, corralled and dominated his prodigious energy, and became the central goal of his personal and professional life.

Audubon compressed into the decade of the 1820s what would be a lifetime's work for most mortals. In travels that ranged from the south to the northeastern regions of the United States, he sought out, discovered, and shot
hundreds of birds, making complete or nearly complete drawings in life size of
most of them. He developed new formats, compositions, media, and techniques
to complement the wide range of birds he encountered, from the smallest songbird to the largest waterfowl. He also worked hard at educating himself through
expanding his social and scientific contacts. Inspired by determination and
necessity, he developed into a successful entrepreneur, finding and enlisting the
support of numerous subscribers to his publication, especially in England during
the latter part of the decade.

Audubon spent most of 1821 in and around New Orleans supporting himself by teaching art and drawing portraits as he had in Ohio. He secured an introduction to the history painter, John Vanderlyn (1775–1852), and showed him a
portfolio of drawings in the hope of securing a written recommendation from
him for a position of draughtsman on a government-sponsored western expedition. Vanderlyn responded to the request with rude disdain. Audubon was asked

to lay his drawings on the dirty floor and wait for the master to look them over. The treatment enraged Audubon and caused him to wonder whether "all Men of Talents are fools and Rude purposely or Naturally?" Audubon, apparently, held his anger to himself and endured treatment that he considered fit for a slave. As a result of his uncharacteristic emotional restraint, he obtained Vanderlyn's approval of his work. The American artist judged Audubon's drawings "handsomely done," with the birds finely colored and in good positions. In Vanderlyn's view, Audubon accomplished a "truth and Accuracy of representation as much so as any I have seen in any Country."[20] Even with the imprimatur of Vanderlyn—a bona fide student of Jacques-Louis David—and letters to Henry Clay and Governor Miller of the Arkansas Territory, no opportunity developed at this time for Audubon to go west and explore his long-imagined Rocky Mountains.

The original watercolor for the etching of *The American Redstart* is inscribed "Drawn from Nature by John James Audubon, Louisiana August 13th 1821" (p. 39). It was made when Audubon and Joseph Mason were living at Oakley Plantation outside New Orleans and shows the developing compositional complexity of Audubon's style with the collaboration of his assistant. A pair of American Redstarts, male and female, are set on adjoining branches of a flowering ironwood tree near an active wasp nest. Under the design direction of Audubon, Mason probably supplied most of the botanical subject, with the graceful curve of the lower branch of the tree providing a stage for the central encounter of the male Redstart with the wasp. Audubon describes the confrontation between bird and insect that he had observed in nature. With beak ajar and wings spread in agitation, the Redstart attempts to capture its prey but is foiled by the protruding sting of the wasp. The natural drama is conveyed by a complex compositional design of interrelated curves. The branches, the wasp's nest, and the leaves of the tree twist and bend in vigorous response to the conflict between the songbird and its adversary—the wasp. Here, as in other later Audubon drawings, one wonders about the symbolic overtones of the image. "In those happy days of my youth," Audubon recalled, "I was extremely fond of reading what I still call the delightful moral fables of La Fontaine."[21] This image recalls a number of fables by the seventeenth-century French writer devoted to the ideas of strength and weakness, and their implicit injunction against making judgments based upon appearances. The stories suggest through their animal protagonists that with intelligence the slow can outpace the fast, the weak can subdue the strong, and the small can defeat the large. La Fontaine's story of "The Lion and the Gnat," which points up the power of a tiny insect to subdue the king of the jungle by buzzing around and driving him to distraction, suggests a possible source for the symbolic implications of Audubon's image. This fable and others of its type were included in the *Fable* cycle's first two volumes, which were dedicated to the Dauphin of France and were intended to instruct princes in the appropriate use of their powers.[22] Whether such political implications survive in Audubon's work remains an intriguing question.[23]

The compositional format that Audubon used for the Redstarts, showing a pair of birds—male and female—decoratively arranged on a botanical support with no landscape setting is one that he developed frequently and with great variety for small and medium-sized birds. In Natchez, Mississippi, in 1822, Audubon delineated a pair of Chuck-will's-widows perched on two dead branches responding to a snake near them. The encounter re-enacts a drama that the ornithologist had observed in nature (p. 42). Although it might be assumed that the birds are frightened by the snake, the reverse is true. The birds are the aggressors. Audubon noted that Chuck-will's-widows often landed purposely near snakes and tried to scare them off by opening their beaks wide and letting forth a frightening hiss. The female bird, perched on the lower branch in this plate, is engaged in just such a dismissing shout. The male joins in the attack, flapping his wings and spreading his tail feathers to create a commotion, thereby enhancing the composition with a brilliant display of pattern in the webs of his plumage. His small, closed bill points directly down at his mate, visually linking the principal protagonists in this natural drama. Audubon misidentified the deadly Coral Snake in this plate as a harmless harlequin. The Chuck-will's-widows' violent response to the poisonous reptile indicates that they knew better.

The exquisite detail and luminous texture that Audubon describes in the intricate patterning of the birds' plumage reflects, in part, the artist's increased use of watercolor, which in his earlier work had been confined to the bills and feet of the birds. The subtle shades of tan, ochre, grey, and black in these nocturnal birds' feathers take on a brilliance and a lightness more evocative of butterflies or moths than of birds. Even the fine bristles at the base of the bill, which the Chuck-will's-widow uses to assist it in capturing its insect-prey, are delineated in watercolor, laid on with a sureness of stroke and delicacy of design. In his desire to achieve a new naturalism in his depiction of birds, Audubon capitalized on the range of touch, texture, and opacity that he could elicit from the watercolor medium, adding pastel, graphite, and gouache for special effects.

A comparison of another bird plate, the *Black-billed Cuckoos*, with the Chuck-will's-widow, and painted in the same year, exposes an inverted balance of bird and plant subjects (p. 43). The Chuck-will's-widows clearly dominate their setting, while the Cuckoos are obscured by the leafy branch of the flowering magnolia tree. Although Audubon did not often acknowledge the botanical contributions of Joseph Mason in the works produced in New Orleans and Mississippi from 1820 to 1822, it is thought that most of the botanical backgrounds for images produced during those years were provided by him. (Mason left Audubon's employ after two years, probably in a huff for just that reason). Mason did claim this exuberant Magnolia as his work, although his signature does not appear on the original watercolor. It is a masterful conception. The flower is depicted in four stages of development—a kind of cycle of life forming a wreath at the center of the composition. At the bottom is a pale green, tightly closed bud, perhaps growing from the same stalk as a luscious, thick, partially opened white bloom at lower right. Its foil—a wilted, overripe flower, denuded of many of its petals—is counterpoised at lower left. An elegant, mature, almost fully opened white magnolia blooms in frontal posture. It projects from the focal center of the plate, with the male and female Cuckoos displayed in heraldic symmetry on

Chuck-will's-widow

Audubon's name: Chuck-will's-widow. 1822. Robert Havell, engraver.
Hand-colored etching and aquatint, 26 × 20½".
New York Public Library.

A member of the nightjar family, the Chuck-will's-widow is nocturnal and spends its days asleep on tree branches, camouflaged by its feather pattern resembling dead leaves. It can be found throughout the river woodlands and pine groves of the southeastern United States. This bird derives its name from its distinctive call of "chuck-will-wid-ow," which is similar to, but slower than, the Whip-poor-will's, to which it is related.

This print is based on a painting completed on May 7, 1822, in Natchez, Mississippi, where Audubon first observed the interaction of Chuck-will's-widows with snakes. "The Chuck-will's-widow manifests a strong antipathy towards all snakes, however harmless they may be. Although these birds cannot in any way injure snakes, they alight near them on all occasions, and try to frighten them away, by opening their prodigious mouth and emitting a strong hissing murmur. It was after witnessing one of these occurrences which took place at early twilight, that the idea of representing these birds in such an occupation struck me. The beautiful little snake, gliding along the dead branch, between two Chuck-will's-widows, a male and a female, is commonly called the Harlequin Snake, and," wrote Audubon confidently, "is, I believe, quite harmless." (Ornithological Biography, 1:276) *Clearly, Audubon should not be considered an authority on snakes, as the one in the print is actually the poisonous coral snake.*

Black-billed Cuckoo

Audubon's name: Black-billed Cuckoo. 1822.
Robert Havell, engraver.
Hand-colored etching and aquatint, 18¾ × 26½".
Collection of The New-York Historical Society.

Today, as in 1822, when Audubon observed and painted the two cuckoos on this plate, the birds are very difficult to locate in Louisiana. The Black-billed Cuckoo has a range that stretches from southern Canada to the central and northeastern United States, and it winters in northern South America. "It being so scarce a species in Louisiana," wrote Audubon, "I have honoured it by placing a pair on a branch of Magnolia in bloom, although the birds represented were not shot on one of these trees, but in a swamp near some, where the birds were in pursuit of such flies as you see figured, probably to amuse themselves." The magnolia branch, showing the blossom of that tree in three different stages of development, may not have been painted by Audubon, but by Joseph Mason, his artist assistant and traveling companion down the Mississippi River and in Louisiana from the fall of 1820 to the summer of 1822. (Ornithological Biography, 1:170–71)

either side of it. The stiff, waxy leaves of the magnolia surround the flowers and birds in a profusion of stages of maturity and decay. There are some lighter green new leaves, some mature deep green shiny specimens, and some lifeless withered brown leaves barely hanging on to the branch. A variety of natural forces have altered the leaves. The wind has forced them into bent and contorted shapes, and insects have torn at their edges, like pinking shears, or punctured their interiors and disrupted the neat pattern of their parallel veins. By no means a snapshot, this drawing of a magnolia can be read as a metaphor for survival. It is not surprising that Audubon was reluctant to acknowledge, or compete with, the contributions of his gifted young assistant.

Audubon rendered all the elements in his picture of the *Greater Prairie Chicken*, including the two male birds apparently fighting over the female, the Turk's Cap Lily, and the landscape background (p. 54). As in all his compositions, the birds appear in the near foreground to show them in large scale and minute detail. These birds enact a mating drama that Audubon witnessed and recorded with great interest in his journal. "It not infrequently happens," he wrote, "that a male already mated is suddenly attacked by some disappointed rival who unexpectedly pounces upon him after a flight of considerable length, having been attracted by the cacklings of the happy couple. The female invariably squats next to and almost under the breast of her lord, while he, always ready for action, throws himself on his daring antagonist, and chases him away never to return. Such is the moment which I have attempted to represent in the plate," he pointed out, and indeed, with that narrative in mind we respond to this image as more than just a visual representation of a particular species of bird.[24]

This image describes Audubon's interpretation of mating in the Greater Prairie Chicken that captured his imagination when he observed it in the wild. The competitive, active encounter of the male birds and the dependent, passive role of the female bird is described in such highly anthropomorphic terms that the role of Audubon as an objective, ornithological observer of nature is called into question. Part of the lively quality of the watercolor derives from the artist's individual engagement in the interpersonal relationships of the male and female birds. The romanticized drama pictured here is underscored by the gestures and the facial expressions of the birds, particularly the eyes. It was Audubon's goal, as he wrote about his particular approach to drawing, to represent, "if possible, each family as if employed in their most constant and natural avocations, and to complete those family pictures as chance might bring perfect specimens."[25] Each plate would constitute a kind of summary family album by recording the generations, the genders, and the characteristic life experiences of its members.

Audubon situated the group of Prairie Chickens in a western meadow setting with a backdrop of hills and mountains, and embellished it with a lily that was environmentally appropriate to the setting. Although all the elements of this watercolor could be observed in one place at one time, it is clear that Audubon does not represent a *plein air* vision of birds and flowers in a landscape. This painting is a composition, not a view; the artist studied and sketched each of the elements separately and later combined them into a single work. This watercolor was probably painted in 1824 in the Great Lakes region, but most of Audubon's observations of the Greater Prairie Chicken were made during his stay in Kentucky, where these birds were in abundance. He noted that the lily grew in swamp areas in the northern, eastern, and western regions of this country. He reduced the stem of this flower, which normally grows to about five feet tall, in order to fit it into the composition. Such adjustments in scale were inevitable to create a pleasing and believable aesthetic totality. However, during his compositional process Audubon never compromised the natural size and the precision of color and markings of his central subject—the birds.

Audubon's touching representation of *Passenger Pigeon* courtship (p. 46), also painted in 1824, acquires special poignancy since the species is now extinct. Once the most numerous bird in North America, numbering in the billions in Kentucky, Ohio, and Indiana, Audubon described with disgust a violent Passenger Pigeon hunting scene that he witnessed in Ohio. Early in the day, farmers arrived at a pigeon roosting site in great numbers with guns and ammunition. Some brought as many as three hundred hogs each, to feed on the remains of the slaughter. The migrating birds began to arrive in the evening in flocks so large that they sounded like "a hard gale at sea." This sound was met and overpowered by a continuous roar of gun reports that extended throughout the night resulting in a mayhem of noise and destruction. At sunrise, when hawks and eagles began to arrive to share in the spoils, "the authors of all this devastation began their entry amongst the dead, the dying and the mangled," Audubon reported. "The pigeons were picked up and piled in heaps, until each had as many as he could possibly dispose of, when the hogs were let loose to feed on the remainder."[26]

In spite of his repulsion at the unnecessary mass killing of the Passenger Pigeon, Audubon misjudged its consequences. The vast quantities of these pigeons and their ability to quadruple their numbers annually, he optimistically thought, would prevent their extinction. He suspected that only the destruction of their habitat, through the gradual diminution of the forests, could seriously threaten the survival of the pigeon. In fact, the combination of both forces—hunting and habitat loss—caused the erasure of the species. The last Passenger Pigeon in captivity died at the Cincinnati Zoo on September 14, 1914.

Audubon was a hunter as well as an ornithologist. He shot birds to secure food, specimens for study, and on a small scale he shot for sport. For him, unnecessary mass shooting was tantamount to murder, an attitude he expressed in his actions and in his writings. A small figure of a hunter with a gun appears in the right distance of Audubon's watercolor of the *Snowy Egret* (p. 47). He is moving forward over a rise in the terrain to get in range of his prey—the slender white "Snowie," as it is often called, with its graceful curves and elegant plumage. Seen as a projection of Audubon as a hunter, this figure was seeking the bird for one of two reasons: either for its flesh, which the artist noted was "excellent eating, especially in early autumn, when it was generally fat"; or for study. He used his specimen to observe its external appearance for painting or to dissect its interior to understand its life habits for his writings.[27] On one occasion, Audubon, who

Passenger Pigeon

Audubon's name: Passenger Pigeon. Painted in Pittsburgh in the autumn of 1824. Robert Havell, engraver.
Hand-colored etching and aquatint, 26 × 20¾".
New York Public Library.

Extinct today, the sheer numbers of Passenger Pigeons in Audubon's time allowed him to make accurate observations of the birds' habits. He noted the bird's speed, which he calculated at three to four hundred miles covered in six hours, and the sharp eyesight that enabled it to spot food while flying high above. Perhaps most interesting are Audubon's observations about the birds' motivation for travel. "The most important facts connected with [the Passenger Pigeon's] habits relate to its migrations," he noted. "These are entirely owing to the necessity of procuring food, and are not performed with a view of escaping the severity of a northern latitude, or of seeking a southern one for the purpose of breeding." (Ornithological Biography, *1:319–320)*

In the drawing on which this print is based, Audubon depicted a pair of Passenger Pigeons during breeding. "The male assumes a pompous demeanour, and follows the female whether on the ground or on the branches, with spread tail and drooping wings, which it rubs against the part over which it is moving. The body is elevated, the throat swells, the eyes sparkle. . . . they caress each other by billing, in which action the bill of one is introduced transversely into that of the other, and both parties alternately disgorge the contents of their crop by repeated efforts." (Ornithological Biography, *1:325) In this image, the female is feeding the male.*

Snowy Egret

Audubon's name: Snowy Heron. Probably painted
on March 25, 1832, in Charleston, SC
Watercolor, graphite, gouache, and selective
scraping on paper, 29¼ × 21⁵⁄₁₆".
Collection of The New-York Historical Society.

*Audubon depicted the Snowy Egret in its
full breeding plumage, which it displays
during courtship in the spring. At the end
of the nesting season, the long plumes are
replaced by short, straight feathers. The
bird was probably painted on March 25,
1832, while Audubon was visiting his
friend John Bachman in Charleston,
South Carolina. "At the approach of the
breeding season," he wrote, "many spend
a great part of the day at their roosting
places, perched on low trees principally
growing in the water, when every now and
then they utter a rough guttural sort of
sigh, raising at the same moment their
beautiful crest and loose recurved plumes,
curving the neck, and rising on their legs
to their full height as if about to strut on
the branches." (*Ornithological Biography, *3:318) George Lehman provided the
landscape setting for the Egret, including
the Charleston skyline to indicate where
Audubon observed the bird.*

*Not surprisingly, the Snowy Egret was
once threatened by extinction because of
the beauty of its plumage, which was
much favored as decoration for ladies'
hats. Protective legislation and perhaps
changes in style have taken the species off
the endangered list.*

Carolina Parakeet

Audubon's name: Carolina Parrot. 1825.
Watercolor, graphite, gouache, crayon/pastel, and
selective glazing on paper, 29¹¹⁄₁₆ × 21³⁄₁₆".
Collection of The New-York Historical Society.

*The colorful Carolina Parakeet is now
extinct and was already being depleted in
Audubon's day. In 1831, he wrote, "Our
Parakeets are rapidly diminishing in
number; and in some districts, where
twenty-five years ago they were plentiful,
scarcely any are now to be seen."*
(Ornithological Biography, 1:138)
*These colorful birds were hunted for their
feathers, captured as pets, and, perhaps
most damagingly, slaughtered as pests by
farmers. "The Parakeets are destroyed in
great numbers, for whilst busily engaged
in plucking off the fruits or tearing the
grain from the stacks, the husbandman
approaches them with perfect ease, and
commits great slaughter among them. . . .
The gun is kept at work . . . until so few
remain alive, that the farmer does not consider it worth his while to spend more of his
ammunition." (Ornithological Biography, 1:136)*

*While Parakeets were unwelcome visi-
tors to the farmer, Audubon appreciated
their merits. "The woods are the habitation
best fitted for them, and there the richness
of their plumage, their beautiful mode of
flight, and even their screams, afford welcome intimation that our darkest forests
and most sequestered swamps are not des-
titute of charms." (Ornithological
Biography, 1:138) Indeed, this colorful
painting, with its portrayal of birds in a
variety of postures, has long been considered one of Audubon's most exceptional
compositions.*

was in search of game, heard the "yelping notes of some gobblers [Wild Turkey] approaching," lured by the presence of a nearby hen. With his gun in hand, he concealed himself behind a fallen tree and watched as about thirty cocks came so close to him that he could see the light in their eyes. He fired one barrel and shot three birds. Instead of flying off in fright, the other cocks started strutting around their fallen companions giving the hunter the opportunity to kill more. "Had I not looked on shooting again as murder without necessity, I might have secured at least another."[28] For this attitude toward purposeless killing, Audubon's name was aptly given to the first conservation society founded in the United States in 1886.

Perhaps ironically, Audubon combined seven examples of another extinct species—the Carolina Parakeet—to form one of his most distinctive images (opposite). "Doubtless, the reader will say, while looking at the seven figures of Parakeets represented in the plate, that I spared not my labour," Audubon remarked, and continued in his ingratiating way, "I never do, so anxious am I to promote his pleasure."[29] Audubon observed with alarm the rapid depletion of the Carolina Parakeet. The only parrot native to the United States, the parakeet succumbed to farmers, who first deprived them of their forest habitats through clearing for cultivation and then shot them in retaliation for eating their crops. Audubon was attracted to the visual display of the parakeets' glorious coloring, which appeared to him as a brilliantly patterned carpet thrown over the stacks of grain on which he watched great numbers of them feeding. To the distinguished English zoologist and artist, William Swainson (1789–1855), who was a friend of Audubon's, the plumage of the Carolina Parakeet held no such appeal. In a complimentary article about the artist and his work published in 1828, Swainson commented that this bird must indeed be a favorite of Audubon's since he included so many of them in the same composition and in spite of their unsuitability for painting. "The superabundant vividness of the golden and red heads of these birds," he remarked with distaste, "defy all attempts at harmonizing."[30]

The birds depicted in this watercolor are perched on the branches of a cocklebur in an S-shaped curve which culminates at the top and the bottom with a flamboyant spread of wing and tail feathers. The active postures of the birds, displayed from all points of view, turning their bodies, twisting their necks, and opening their beaks, create a visual "din" of activity comparable to the cacophony of their screams. The expressive character of Audubon's parakeets has been compared to ancient Chinese bird and flower paintings. Audubon shares in the Oriental aesthetic goal of capturing "the idea and not merely the shape" of the subject. Thus, in this painting of the parakeets, Audubon reaches beyond the literal transcription of the surface of the bird to convey its inner aliveness.[31]

Sometimes Audubon combined numerous examples of the same species of bird on a single page for dramatic rather than aesthetic effect. In the *Mockingbird*, he describes an aggressive attack by a rattlesnake on a Northern Mockingbird nest, an event that some critics considered a fantasy on the part of Audubon (p. 59). A flowering yellow jasmine supports four mockingbirds and an egg-filled

Ruffed Grouse

Audubon's name: Ruffed Grouse. 1824. Robert Havell, engraver.
Hand-colored etching and aquatint, 25¼ × 38¾".
New York Public Library.

In delineating the Ruffed Grouse, Audubon exposed to scrutiny a bird that is rarely seen unless flushed from a thicket. "On the ground, where the Ruffed Grouse spends a large portion of its time, its motions are peculiarly graceful," the artist observed. "It walks with an elevated firm step, opening its beautiful tail gently and with a well-marked jet, holding erect its head, the feathers of which are frequently raised, as are the velvety tufts of its neck. It poises its body on one foot for several seconds at a time, and utters a soft cluck, which in itself implies a degree of confidence in the bird that its tout ensemble is deserving of the notice of any bystander." (Ornithological Biography, 1:213)

In his drawing, Audubon presented a female below two males, reaching for the berries of the moonseed plant. The males are shown from front and back, fully displaying their elegant coloration. The Ruffed Grouse, which is present in Alaska, Canada, and the northern United States, has two color morphs, red-brown and gray-brown. Audubon, who drew the birds in Pennsylvania or New York, has depicted the red birds, which are more common in the area.

nest, which is enwrapped in the coils of the snake. His jaw opens wide exposing his threatening fangs to the bird at lower left, whose wings are spread in alarm. All the other birds respond in some way to the central confrontation between bird and reptile. Conflict in nature, a theme that appears in many of Audubon's images, is the focus of this watercolor. The artist's legendary ability as a storyteller takes precedence, in this composition, over clarity and elegance of design. While some scientists disputed the ability of rattlesnakes to climb trees, others, such as William Swainson, delighted in elaborating on the story that Audubon suggests in the image:

The formidable reptile has driven the female bird from her eggs, which he intends to suck. Unable to defend them while sitting, she clings to the side; . . . Her cries have brought two others of her race to the spot: but these, not feeling a parent's solicitude, 'come not boldly' to the attack. On the courage of the male bird the fate of the conflict seems to depend. He is close to the serpent, aiming a deadly stroke at its eye, while his own is lighted up with a determination and courage, which seem to bespeak anticipated victory. Every part of the story is told with exquisite feeling.[32]

During the mid-1820s, Audubon employed a range of compositions for his bird paintings. In the same year, 1825, that Audubon included ten *Ruby-throated Hummingbirds* (p. 60) flitting about the blossoms on branches of a trumpet-creeper, he also produced his signature image of a single *Wild Turkey* standing majestically on a marshy reeded ground (p. 61). The artist assigned to the Wild Turkey a place of honor as Plate I in his publication of *The Birds of America.* Standing in the contrapposto posture of a classical Greek sculpture, this large male bird, an American native, strides through the cane and grass setting with authority. Once favored as the national symbol of America, the wild turkey ceded that position to the Bald Eagle, but, at least in Audubon's mind, lost none of its dignity in the process. The larger-than-life presence of Audubon's turkey is magnified when compared with Titian Peale's rendering of the same species for Alexander Wilson's *American Ornithology* (p. 29). Peale's turkey cock, shown together with a hen, appears in strict profile, which creates a stylized and static design. It lacks the taut animation that the twisted neck lends Audubon's bird.

The actual size of Audubon's turkey drawing, which is more than ten times larger than Peale's—an enlargement that measures Audubon's ambition to supplant the accomplishment of the earlier ornithologist—is further enhanced by the dominant presence of the bird on the page. Audubon's turkey cock fills the sheet, and the contours of the bird touch the edges on all four sides of the paper. The majestic fowl stands erect and disposes its considerable weight on the ground. The companion image of the hen and chicks similarly dominates the page. The text accompanying Peale's engraving, which was edited after Wilson's death by Charles L. Bonaparte (1803–1857) indicates that the looming presence of Audubon as a rival artist and ornithologist continued long after Wilson's death in 1813. "The natural history of the turkey is so well and fully detailed by our author [Alexander Wilson]," argued Bonaparte, "that almost nothing can

Common Eider

Audubon's name: Eider Duck. 1833. Robert Havell, engraver.
Hand-colored etching and aquatint, 25½ × 38¾".
New York Public Library.

During his 1833 trip to Labrador, Audubon had ample opportunity to view and examine Common Eiders, which were breeding in large numbers along the coast. "The Eider Ducks are seen leaving the islands on which they breed, at daybreak every fair morning, in congregated flocks of males and females separately," Audubon noted of their daily habits in his journal on June 20th. "They proceed to certain fishing grounds where the water is only a few fathoms deep, and remain till towards evening, when the females sit on their eggs for the night, and the males group on the rocks by themselves. This valuable bird is extremely abundant here; we find their nests without any effort every time we go out." (Journals, 1:372)

The abundance of the ducks and their nests allowed Audubon to record detailed observations about them. "The nests were scooped a few inches deep in the mossy, rotten substance that forms here what must be called earth," wrote the naturalist. "The eggs are deposited on a bed of down and covered with the same material; and so warm are these nests that, although not a parent bird was seen near them, the eggs were quite warm to the touch, and the chicks in some actually hatching in the absence of the mother." (Journals, 1:366–367) Audubon's scientific objectivity was, at times, paired with more affectionate and personal observations of the bird: "the Eider Duck swimming man-of-war-like amid her floating brood, like the guardship of a most valuable convoy." (Journals, 1:387) In this print, Audubon represents the birds in dramatic conflict. A mated pair vigorously responds to the intrusion of another male into their nesting place.

be added, even from the later observations of Audubon."[33]

Audubon's representation of the national bird of the United States, the *Bald Eagle* (p. 63), shares some of the majesty of the *Wild Turkey*. It also reflects some of the artist's preoccupation with nature as a repository for moral lessons. Benjamin Franklin judged that the moral character of the Bald Eagle made it unsuitable as the national standard and Audubon shared similar reservations. In Audubon's watercolor, the bird is shown standing on a rocky support gripping a catfish prey in its talons. An exultant glint in its eye seems to express emotional pleasure in response to the success of its conquest. To understand Audubon's perception of this predatory behavior, we must consider the various ways in which he judged the bird. Audubon, a staunch loyalist to his adopted United States, called the eagle a "noble bird" and praised its strength, daring, and courage. As the national standard, the bird was symbolically responsible, in his view, for "bearing to distant lands the remembrance of a great people living in a state of peaceful freedom."[34] To that positive assertion, Audubon added, "May that peaceful freedom last for ever!" Perhaps the predatory qualities, which Audubon acknowledged were given to this wild species by the Creator "to enable him to perform the office assigned to him," could be understood also as moral lessons for civilized man. The *Bald Eagle* could simultaneously represent a model of courageous behavior, suitable in nature, and a warning against such rapacious behavior in society, with its implicit threat to peace and freedom.

Audubon did not articulate specific symbolic agendas underpinning his drawings when he sat down to write about the aesthetic and scientific goals that guided his work. His 1826 "Account of the Method of Drawing Birds," which was published two years later in the *Edinburgh Journal of Science*, illuminates some of the principles that guided his approach to illustrating birds. "My wish to impart truths has been my guide in every instance," asserted Audubon; "all the observations respecting them [the birds] are my own."[35] Fundamental to Audubon's approach to nature was his desire to capture a new kind of truth: one that could only be gained through the immediacy of firsthand experience. He set out to acquire intimate knowledge of both the appearance and life habits of birds through careful observation during repeated encounters. He would not rely on the images or written descriptions of American birds by earlier ornithologists since, he judged, many of them were based upon secondhand information or stuffed specimens.

"Nature *must* be seen first alive, and well studied," wrote Audubon, "before attempts are made at representing it."[36] The artist's extensive travels through the United States, sometimes requiring years of separation from his beloved family, brought him an unmatched familiarity with his treasured objects through intimate study in the wild. From this familiarity, he developed the conviction that isolating a single specimen of bird and depicting it from a profile point of view, which was typical of most earlier bird drawings, did not represent "nature as it existed," or at least as Audubon experienced it.

He thought it important to include female and young birds along with the mature male. This would make it possible to avoid mistaking the female, or

Greater Prairie Chicken

Audubon's Name: Pinnated Grouse. 1824.
Watercolor on paper, 25 × 35⅞″ (sight).
Collection of The New-York Historical Society.

*Having depicted in this watercolor a male
Greater Prairie Chicken defending himself
and his mate against a jealous rival,
Audubon also described the distinctive
mating ritual or battle of the male birds:
"Their tails are spread out and inclined
forwards, to meet the expanded feathers of
their neck, which now, like stiffened frills,
lie supported by the globular orange-
coloured receptacles of air, from which
their singular booming sounds proceed
. . . at the very first answer from some coy
female, the heated blood of the feathered
warriors swells every vein, and presently
the battle rages."* (Ornithological Biography, 2:492–3)

*When Audubon first observed this bird
in the Barrens of Kentucky, it was so plentiful that a friend of his killed forty in one
morning, declining to pick even one up
because he was tired of eating them. By the
1830s, there was scarcely one to be found,
most of the Prairie Chickens having abandoned Kentucky "to escape from the mur-
derous white man."* (Ornithological
Biography, 2:491) *Audubon, who tried
to faithfully depict the vegetation and
landscape of the Barrens of Kentucky in
this drawing, later reminisced about the
early years he had spent there: "There it
was, that, year after year, and each succes-
sive season, I studied the habits of the Pin-*

nated Grous (sic). *It was there that, before
sunrise, or at the close of the day, I heard
its curious boomings, witnessed its obsti-
nate battles, watched it during the
progress of its courtships, noted its nest
and eggs, and followed its young until,
fully grown, they betook themselves to their
winter quarters."* (Ornithological Biography, 2:491)

immature, forms of a single species for members of another. Thus his many compositions, including male and female pairs, and those depicting numerous birds of the same species in different stages of development, conformed to his view of a comprehensive projection of nature through the artist's complex lens.

To capture accurately the vigorous appearance of the birds that he observed in nature, Audubon invented techniques and methods to support his goal. As specimens, he chose only birds that were freshly killed, preferably by his own gun. In this state, he could quickly wire them to an apparatus which he called a "position board" that he invented to hold them in lifelike postures. In this manner, he avoided the stiff, unnatural profile portraits that could not be observed in nature. With wires and tiny metal skewers, the artist could fix the feet on a board in an active posture, suspend the wings and tail feathers in a flight position, twist the head and open the beak to let out a soundless call. With his fingers, he would press aside the eyelids of the fresh-killed bird to reveal an eye which still retained its vivid color and luminosity.

For Audubon, recreating the natural size of every bird was critical to his conception of a truthful image. He wanted to represent each bird in its exact length and breadth and with all of its parts in precise proportion as "they existed in nature." To that end, in his words, he "copied with a closeness of measurement that I hope will always correspond with nature when brought into close contact."[37] Audubon's pencil drawing for the *Audubon's Shearwater* and many of his watercolors contain precise inscriptions of measurements of many parts of the birds' bodies taken with rulers and compasses that were part of the tools of his trade (p. 65). In the lower left hand corner of the *Shearwater* drawing, the artist penciled in the following measurements: "Total length, 11 Inches; Tail extent beyond wings closed ¹⁄₁₂; Breadth 2 feet 2½–12." To the right of the birds, tucked into notes about the color of the bird and the quality of its tongue, he inscribed "above [bird is] Size of Life" in emphatic capital letters.

Audubon placed a grid or a graph behind his specimen and one on his sheet, in the manner of a Renaissance artist, to accurately record the proportions of the parts to the whole in his renderings of birds in actual size. To embrace these perfectly scaled birds on paper, Audubon employed three different sizes of sheets. The small songbirds appeared on the approximately 11 by 18 inch sheets, the midsized birds appeared on the 19 by 26 inch sheets, and the large water birds required the 25 by 38 inch sheets and sometimes had to bend in order to fit.

Audubon had developed into a mature and original painter of birds, an achievement that had depended upon a long apprenticeship in the woods. Separated from engagement in society, which his skills as a musician, dancer, and raconteur had previously made so enjoyable, he adapted to a more "solitary state of habits," with no more than one or two companions at his side. Indeed, this mercurial man gradually came to prefer the natural state. "I am persuaded that alone in the woods, or at my work," he claimed, "I can make better use of the whole of my self than in any other situation, and that thereby I have lost nothing in exchanging the pleasure of studying men for that of admiring the feathered race."[38] Audubon had assumed so effectively the role of Natty Bumpo, the

Joseph Bartholomew Kidd
(1808–1889), after John James
Audubon. *Carolina Parakeet*

1831. Oil on canvas, 25⅞ × 38⅜″.
Courtesy, Department of Library Services,
American Museum of Natural History, New York.

*Audubon met Joseph B. Kidd, a young
landscape painter, during his visit to
Edinburgh in 1827. At that time, Kidd
added backgrounds to several of Audubon's new oil copies of his watercolors of
birds. The following year, Kidd became
Audubon's pupil in London, and in
1831, Audubon engaged him to make oil
copies of all his watercolors. Only some of
the copies were completed. Among them is
this oil painting of the* Carolina Parakeet *(1831). The foliage in the background does not appear in the watercolor
or the engraving of this work.*

Fork-tailed Flycatcher

Audubon's name: Forked-tailed Flycatcher. 1832.
Watercolor, graphite, and gouache on paper,
21½ × 14¹⁄₁₆".
Collection of The New-York Historical Society.

*Audubon made this drawing in June
1832 from a bird he had just killed near
Camden, New Jersey. "It lived only a few
minutes [after being wounded]," he wrote,
"and from it the drawing transferred to
the plate was made. . . . The bird has been
placed on a plant which grows in Georgia,
and which was drawn by my friend Bachman's sister [Maria Martin]." He
observed the Fork-tailed Flycatcher in
flight before shooting it: "While on the
wing, it frequently employed its long tail,
when performing sudden turns in following its prey, and when alighted, it vibrated
it in the manner of the Sparrow-Hawk."*
(Ornithological Biography, 2:387)
*Audubon was fortunate to procure the
specimen, as the bird is indigenous to
South America and is rarely seen in the
United States.*

Alexander Wilson (1766–1813).
*Carolina Parrot. Canada Flycatcher.
Hooded Flycatcher. Green Black-Capt
Flycatcher*

c. 1811. Hand-colored etching, 8¾ × 5½".
Engraved by W. H. Lizars. From A. Wilson, *American
Ornithology; or The Natural History of the Birds of the
United States*, Vol. 1, Plate 26 (page 376).
New York Public Library.

*"Of one hundred and sixty-eight kinds of
parrots enumerated by European writers
as inhabiting the various regions of the
globe,"* wrote Alexander Wilson, *"this is
the only species found native within the
territory of the United States. The vast
and luxuriant tracts lying within the tor-
rid zone, seem to be the favourite residence
of those noisy, numerous, and richly
plumaged tribes."* (American Ornithology; or, The Natural History of the
Birds of the United States, *3 vols.
[London: Whittaker, Treacher, & Arnot,
1832], 1:376–377) Unfortunately, the
Carolina Parakeet, once so numerous, is
now extinct. The last authenticated sighting of the bird occurred in Florida in
1920. Wilson was impressed by the native
American parakeet's "elegance of figure
and beauty of plumage," in comparison to
similar birds from foreign countries, as
well as its nature and abilities: "It is alike
docile and sociable; soon becomes perfectly
familiar; and, until equal pains be taken
in its instruction, it is unfair to conclude
it incapable of equal improvement [to that
of paraakeets from abroad] in the lan-
guage of man."* (American Ornithology, *1:383*)

1. *Carolina Parrot.* 2. *Canada Flycatcher.* 3. *Hooded F.* 4. *Green black-capt F.*
26

mythic, frontier hero of James Fenimore Cooper's 1823 Leatherstocking novel,
The Pioneers, that he had virtually merged his identity with the character. Cooper
was one of Audubon's favorite authors.

By 1825, he had assembled a portfolio of work large enough to submit for
inspection to subscribers who could help underwrite the completion and publication of *The Birds of America*. The difficulties of that task required that Audubon
rediscover his social persona and invent an entrepreneurial one to achieve
success.

Mocking Bird. TURDUS POLYGLOTTUS. Linn. *Males 1. Females, 2.* Florida jessamine Gelsemium nitidum

Northern Mockingbird

Audubon's name: Mocking Bird. 1825. Robert Havell, engraver.
Hand-colored etching and aquatint, 33¼ × 23¾″.
New York Public Library.

Although this painting was criticized for inaccuracy at the time of its publication in 1827, its critics claiming that rattlesnakes do not climb trees or have outward-curving tips on their fangs, Audubon was actually correct in his depiction. In spite of representing the mockingbird here in violent confrontation, however, Audubon usually associated the bird in harmony with its surroundings. With pangs of homesickness during an extended trip to Europe, he wrote in 1826 in Edinburgh, "never before did I so long for a glimpse of our rich magnolia woods . . . could I be there but a moment, hear the mellow Mock-bird, or the Wood-thrush, to me, always pleasing, how happy should I be; but alas! I am far from those scenes." (Journals, 1:193)

The French painter, François Gerard expressed particular appreciation for this image of the mockingbird, on October 1, 1828, in Paris. "The book opened accidentally at the plate of the Parrots, and Gerard, taking it up without speaking, looked at it . . . with as keen an eye as my own, for several minutes; put it down, took up the one of the Mocking-Birds, and, offering me his hand, said: 'Mr. Audubon, you are the king of ornithological painters,'" Audubon was not hesitant to repeat. "'We are all children in France and in Europe. Who would have expected such things from the woods of America?' My heart thrilled with pride at his words." (Journals, 1:330–331)

Ruby-throated Hummingbird

Audubon's name: Ruby-Throated Humming Bird.
1825. Robert Havell, engraver.
Hand-colored etching and aquatint, 26 × 20½".
New York Public Library.

"Where is the person," Audubon asked, "who, on seeing this lovely little creature moving on humming winglets through the air, suspended as if by magic in it flitting from one flower to another, with motions as graceful as they are light and airy . . . : where is the person . . . who on observing this glittering fragment of the rainbow, would not pause, admire and instantly turn his mind with reverence toward the Almighty Creator . . . ?" (Ornithological Biography, 1:248)

Audubon shared his contemporaries' fascination with this diminutive and pugnacious bird. He found the specimens shown here in 1825 in Louisiana. "I have represented ten of these pretty and most interesting birds in various positions, flitting, feeding, caressing each other, or sitting on the slender stalks of the trumpet-flower and pluming themselves. The diversity of action and attitude thus exhibited, may, I trust, prove sufficient to present a faithful idea of their appearance and manners." (Ornithological Biography, 1:253)

Wild Turkey

Audubon's name: Wild Turkey. c.1825.
Watercolor, pastel, oil, and graphite on paper,
39¼ × 26¼".
Collection of The New-York Historical Society.

The adult male turkey in this watercolor was probably painted in 1825 in West Feliciana Parish, Louisiana. It is shown against a background of cane, suggestive of the riverbanks of the southern United States.

"The great size and beauty of the Wild Turkey, its value as a delicate and highly prized article of food, and the circumstance of its being the origin of the domestic race now generally dispersed over both continents, render it one of the most interesting of the birds indigenous to the United States of America." (Ornithological Biography, *1:1*) *With these opening lines, Audubon began his five-volume* Ornithological Biography, *detailing the appearance and habits of the birds of North America. The Wild Turkey was an appropriate choice to introduce the series, because of its identification with the United States. This bird had strong support in the competition to choose America's national symbol. It lost the position to the Bald Eagle.*

John Abbott (1751–c. 1840).
Ruby-throated Hummingbird

c. 1810. Watercolor and graphite on paper,
12½ × 10".
By permission of the Department of Printing and
Graphic Arts, the Houghton Library, Harvard
University.

This illustration of the Ruby-throated Hummingbird, c. 1810, is unique among John Abbott's works in its display of the bird in flight. While the male perches on a branch surveying the stylized landscape, the female feeds from the trumpet flower near their nest.

Bald Eagle

Audubon's name: White-headed Eagle. 1828.
Watercolor, pastel, graphite, selective glazing, and
selective scraping on paper, 25⅜ × 38¼".
Collection of The New-York Historical Society.

Aware that the Bald Eagle was the national bird of his beloved adopted America, Audubon indulged in romantic superlatives when he described this noble bird. Asking the reader to imagine floating down the Mississippi River and suddenly arriving at this scene, Audubon wrote, "the eagle is seen perched, in an erect attitude, on the highest summit of the tallest tree by the margin of the broad stream. His glistening but stern eye looks over the vast expanse." At that moment, a swan passes nearby and excites the eagle's natural instincts. "The male bird, in full preparation for the chase, starts from his perch with an awful scream. . . . He glides through the air like a falling star, and, like a flash of lightning, comes upon the timorous quarry . . . he presses down his powerful feet, and drives his sharp claws deeper than ever into the heart of the dying Swan. He shrieks with delight, as he feels the last convulsions of his prey." (Ornithological Biography 1:160–161)

This painting, which Audubon completed in London in 1828, is a copy of his original depiction of a Bald Eagle, drawn in 1820 from a specimen shot near Little Prairie, Missouri. In the later work, Audubon has substituted a catfish for the goose that had been the eagle's prey.

American Robin

Audubon's name: American Robin or Migratory
Thrush. 1829. Robert Havell, engraver.
Hand-colored etching and aquatint, 38 × 25¼".
New York Public Library.

*In this image, drawn in 1829 in Great
Egg Harbor, New Jersey, an adult American Robin is shown feeding its young. The
birds' lively depiction in various positions
and the detailed background of the chestnut oak branch contrast with the stiff projection of Audubon's 1807 drawing.*

*Despite the nuisance posed by robins
feeding on berries and fruit from country
fields and farms to city gardens, Audubon
retained great affection for the birds.
"Many people," he wrote in his journal in
1827 while visiting England, "tell me in
cold blood that we have no birds that can
sing in America. . . . What would they say
of a half-million of robins about to take
their departure for the North, making our
woods fairly tremble with melodious harmony?"* (Journals, 1:245–246)

American Robin.
TURDUS MIGRATORIUS.
Male 1. Female 2. Young 3.
Chestnut oak. Quercus Prinos.

PLATE CXXXI

Audubon's Shearwater

Audubon's name: Dusky Petrel. 1826.
Pencil on paper, 7¾ × 12⅛″.
The Beinecke Rare Book and Manuscript Library,
Yale University, New Haven, Connecticut.

*This drawing was made on June 26, 1826, on a ship becalmed off the coast of Florida, giving Audubon ample opportunity to study the flight and feeding patterns of the Shearwater that was later named after the naturalist. Audubon watched these birds he termed "Dusky Petrels" as they skimmed over the water "in search of what is here called Gulf Weed, of which there are large patches, perhaps half an acre in extent. They flap the wings six or seven times, then soar for three or four seconds, the tail spread, the wings extended. Four or five of these birds, indeed sometimes as many as fifteen or twenty, will alight on this weed, dive, flutter, and swim with all the gayety of ducks on a pond, which they have reached after a weary journey." From a specimen shot by the mate on the ship, Audubon dissected the bird's stomach, which he found "much distended by the contents, which were a compound of fishes of different kinds, some almost entire, others more or less digested." (*Journals, *1:89*) This drawing served as a model for the engraving of a Dusky Petrel by Robert Havell in* The Birds of America.

III. Entrepreneur and Writer

Victor and John W. Audubon.
John James Audubon

1841. Oil on canvas, 44 × 60".
Courtesy, Department of Library Services,
American Museum of Natural History, New York.

In 1841, when John and Victor Audubon painted this quintessential portrait of their father, the Audubon family was living a life of relative ease and tranquillity. Audubon had completed his principal work, The Birds of America. *In 1841, he bought the thirty-five acre tract that they named Minnie's Land and that was to be the family estate for over twenty years (until after the artist's death in 1851). While he was never wealthy, Audubon was able to write to his friend John Bachman in 1843, just after his return from his expedition along the upper Missouri River, that he was again "in the lap of comfort and without the hard and continued exercises so lately my lot." (Audubon-Bachman Correspondence, November 12, 1843, Minnie's Land, bMSAm1482, Houghton Library, Harvard University—quoted in Annette Blaugrund, "The Artist as Entrepreneur," in Blaugrund and Stebbins, eds.,* John James Audubon: The Watercolors for the Birds of America *[New York: Random House and the New-York Historical Society, 1993], 41)*

I reached Philadelphia on the 5th April 1824. Just as the Sun left the Horizon—at the exception of the good Doctor Mease whom had visited me in my Boyish days I had scarce an acquaintance—I called on him, shewed a portion of my Drawings—he presented me to C. L. Bonaparte!—how often I have hailed the name—how often have I been grateful & thankful to that learned Naturalist in my heart for the new light he gave to my eyes and to my Senses, when he first said with an open countenance, praising my Illustrations, give them to the World.[39]

With these dramatic words, Audubon suggested that it was Charles Lucien Bonaparte, a twenty-one-year-old naturalist and the nephew of Napoleon, who, in 1824, first gave him the idea of publishing his drawings of birds. Audubon contended that he had no more practical objective than "to enjoy the Works of Nature, no, no other object." He spent the better part of the four previous years traveling extensively far from his family, whom he left with little source of support. As if the point were not clear enough, he repeated, "all those years were spent without thinking of the result. I mean to say that never for a minute did I indulge in the Hope of becoming at all useful to my kind."[40] It is tempting to suggest that he protests too vigorously. With his urgent financial needs, how could Audubon, a responsible man, undertake such a time-consuming project as *The Birds of America* with no practical goal in mind?

Perhaps this denial of a professional objective for his drawings stemmed from a desire to portray himself as an amateur pursuing nature with a purity of spirit untainted by financial considerations. He required the discovery and encouragement of his work by an outsider of some reputation to believe in himself and aim toward a higher goal. As earlier in his life, he had claimed Jacques-Louis David to have been his artistic mentor to legitimize his artistic productions, he now enlisted C. L. Bonaparte's stamp of approval to validate the seriousness of his scientific goal.

Unfortunately for Audubon, even the stewardship of Napoleon's nephew was not entirely sufficient to smooth the way for him through the influential circles of Philadelphia. The center of American science and culture in the 1820s, Philadelphia was the logical place for Audubon to find a talented engraver for his bird drawings and financial support in the form of subscriptions to his publication. Although Bonaparte made it possible for Audubon to exhibit examples of his work at the Philadelphia Academy of Natural Sciences and provided introductions to distinguished engravers, Audubon ran head on into opposition to his work based upon rivalry.

A member of the Philadelphia Academy, George Ord (1781–1866), took immediate dislike to Audubon, and became a long-standing critic of both the artist and his drawings. Ord had collaborated with Alexander Wilson on the early volumes of *American Ornithology* and had completed the work after the author's death. His vested interest in the success of that work and subsequent editions of it made him a natural adversary of Audubon, whose *The Birds of America* would compete directly with the earlier publication. Alexander Lawson, who had been Wilson's engraver and was collaborating on a publication with C. L. Bonaparte, could not be persuaded by his collaborator to find any merit in Audubon's work. Lawson refused even to engrave the drawings that Bonaparte had purchased from the artist, because he judged them "ill drawn, not true to nature and anatomically incorrect" and therefore not worthy of his engraver's burin.[41]

Audubon's flamboyant personal style and occasionally haughty manner further alienated his opponents, who contemptuously dubbed him "the trader naturalist." He fixed his long unruly hair with bear grease and sported pantaloons and a black frock coat (or sometimes a wolf skin), presenting a bizarre frontier appearance that Philadelphians found unseemly (p. 67). Moreover, his claims of birth on American soil and training by French masters echoed in suspicious ears. Their doubts about Audubon's pedigree coupled with their distaste for his self-promotion caused some Philadelphians to judge him harshly. William Dunlap, an artist and writer who published a multivolume work on the development of the arts in the United States in 1834, preferred the modesty of Alexander Wilson and his small-scale work to the bravado of Audubon and his life-sized drawings. "How much science gains by increasing the picture of a bird beyond that size necessary to display all the parts distinctly," he mused, "is with me questionable." Wilson, said Dunlap, managed to contribute a great deal to ornithology "without having his hand guided by David and many masters," and without claiming to be an American when he wasn't.[42]

Happily, this mean-spirited rivalry on the part of some members of Philadelphia's cultural community was mitigated by the friendship and support of others. Edward Harris (1799–1863), a naturalist from New Jersey, bought all of the drawings that Audubon showed him at their first meeting and became a lifelong friend, advisor, and patron. Harris accompanied Audubon on his trip through the southern states to Florida in 1837, and on the Missouri River expedition of 1843. The portrait painter Thomas Sully (1783–1872) also recognized Audubon's talent and admired the drawings shown him when Audubon visited Philadelphia in 1824. At Audubon's request, Sully gave him instruction in the use of oils over a period of about four months, so that Audubon might develop his portrait painting technique in that medium to supplement his income.

In 1822, Audubon had taken his first lessons in oil painting from the itinerant portrait painter John Steen (or Stein), who had also taught the landscape painter Thomas Cole (1801–1848) early on in the Hudson River painter's career in Steubenville, Ohio. Audubon collaborated with Steen on a number of oil portraits in Natchez, Mississippi, and completed some others independently in Louisiana during the early 1820s. He was commissioned by the widow Mrs.

Robert Percy of Beechwoods plantation in West Feliciana, Louisiana, to paint the portraits of her two daughters, who were pupils of Audubon's wife, Lucy. When Mrs. Percy criticized the jaundiced pallor of her daughters' portrait complexions, the novice oil painter reacted with such a temper tantrum that he was thrown off the property. This incident, having taken place shortly before his arrival in Philadelphia, probably prompted Audubon to solicit the talents of the accomplished Sully for further instruction in oils, and perhaps also, working with patrons. "Sully was a man after my own heart," wrote Audubon, "who showed me great kindness. He was a beautiful singer and an artist whose hints and advice [in oil painting] were of great service to me."[43]

Although oils never suited Audubon's artistic sensibility as much as the mixed-media of his works on paper, his improved facility in this medium proved useful during his years abroad. In 1826, Audubon left his family in Louisiana and sailed for England and did not return until 1829. His principal goals were to find an engraver for his bird drawings and to make contacts who could support his publication project. He set off with a small amount of savings from his portrait sales and art teaching, but he needed money to cover his living and traveling expenses almost immediately on his arrival. For income, he made watercolor and oil copies of his bird drawings, which he offered for sale. The latter medium proved the more profitable. At first he painted oils as gifts for friends who offered him lodging and introductions. One version of the *Entrapped Otter* (p. 72) was made for his loyal British patron Mrs. William Rathbone. Later he painted oils on a grander scale, selecting hunting scenes favored by British collectors to promote his reputation and to support his stay abroad while seeking subscribers to *The Birds of America*. Referring probably to an oil painting based upon his image of a Wild Turkey hen and her brood, Audubon marveled, in a letter to Sully in 1826, at the success of his birds amplified by medium, size (57 by 93 inches), and number to fit the paneled library wall of an English country house. "Think of my painting oil pieces of eleven wild turkeys estimated at 100 guineas," he wrote with astonishment, and almost more remarkably "finished in ten days work"[44] (p. 71).

Audubon's principal use of the oil medium, while in England, was to make copies of his bird drawings. The sale of these oils could support the publication of his engravings and help defray his personal expenses. The task proved daunting so he hired Joseph B. Kidd (1808–1889), a young Edinburgh landscape painter to supply the backgrounds. Later, Audubon decided to have Kidd make oil copies of all the engraved plates for *The Birds of America*, a project that was never completed. The *Pileated Woodpecker* (p. 73; cf. p. 83) and the *Carolina Parakeet* are two examples of Kidd's work and the backgrounds in these paintings show the imprint of the younger artist since they do not appear in the watercolor or engraved versions of the same images by Audubon.

Audubon had left for Europe armed with distinguished letters of introduction from Henry Clay, DeWitt Clinton, Andrew Jackson, Thomas Sully, and others. One of the most helpful contacts that his letters of introduction provided Audubon was the Quaker Rathbone family of Liverpool. A pencil and charcoal self-portrait by Audubon (p. 74) and the oil painting *Otter in the Trap* were made as tokens of the artist's appreciation of the many kindnesses the Rathbones showed him. Mrs. William Rathbone and her two sons, Richard and William, part of a wealthy merchant family that was the first to import American baled cotton into Britain, became staunch champions of Audubon and his work. They gave him introductions to important scientists and patrons of the arts and paved the way to such influential subscribers as Lord Stanley, the fourteenth earl of Derby, and William Roscoe (1755–1831), an abolitionist, historian, and botanist. Less than two weeks after Audubon's arrival in Liverpool, Roscoe arranged for him to exhibit, at the Liverpool Royal Institution, over two hundred of the drawings he had brought with him. Audubon counted 413 people in a two-hour attendance period at the exhibition's opening day and subsequent newspaper commentaries applauded the work.[45]

Audubon's successful reception in Liverpool was followed by an even greater one in Edinburgh. He gathered the support of Professor Robert Jameson, an eminent Scottish naturalist who rounded up influential residents and made it possible for Audubon to exhibit his work at the Royal Institution there. Here Audubon became a direct beneficiary of the cash receipts of this well-attended exhibition. An invitation to attend a meeting of the Wernerian Society at the University of Edinburgh, and his subsequent election as a member of that august group, shows that Audubon was beginning to be embraced in scholarly circles as well as social ones. Exhilarated by the welcome and respect he received abroad, Audubon expressed his delight in a letter to Sully. "The newspapers, the people, the nobility, all have paid me homage due only to very superior men, and to tell you that I feel greatly elevated is only a slender way of expressing the grateful feelings that swell my heart," he wrote, "and if I do not become a proud fool (and God forbid) I cannot help but succeed."[46]

Apparently, even Audubon's eccentric appearance and style of dress were appreciated abroad. The artist claimed that this acceptance was the mark of a broad-minded, learned society. So taken with the artist and his engaging look were some of his new Scottish friends, that they insisted Audubon sit for a portrait which could be engraved and distributed abroad. Deeply flattered by the request, Audubon wrote to Lucy in America, "What thinkst thou when it is unanimously agreed that I must set for my portrait . . . ? Next week there will be two Audubons in Edinburgh."[47] A pupil of Sir Henry Raeburn (1756–1823), John Syme (1795–1861) was selected for the task. He represented the forty-one-year-old Audubon as a kind of gallant frontiersman (frontispiece). Dressed in fur-trimmed hunting attire and holding a rifle across his chest, with his dark hair flowing to his shoulders, Audubon takes on the persona of a nineteenth-century Robin Hood gazing wistfully at his cherished but quickly disappearing natural surroundings. "Yet with all this, believe me, a dear thought never leaves me a moment," Audubon assured Sully. "I think constantly of my beloved America and of my friends there."[48]

It was in Edinburgh that Audubon was introduced to William Home Lizars (1788–1859), an expert engraver who would undertake to transfer to copper

ENTREPRENEUR AND WRITER

English Pheasants Surprised by a Dog (Sauve Qui Peut)

1827. Oil on canvas, 57 × 93″.
The Racquet and Tennis Club, New York.

Audubon began to use oil paints in 1822, receiving his first instruction from an itinerant portrait painter named John Steen in Natchez, Mississippi. During his visit to Edinburgh in 1827, he made oil copies of several of his watercolors of birds, and while in London in 1828 he turned to oils once again. Ultimately, Audubon was to find the medium of oil and the grinding of colors tedious and time-consuming.

Responding to the preferences of his English audience, Audubon adapted his natural history subjects to the genre of the British hunting scene. Conceived as a grand work in that tradition, English Pheasants Surprised by a Dog (Sauve qui Peut) *was begun in December 1826 on a large canvas, depicting a covey of fourteen pheasants startled by a fox. Eventually, disappointed with the fox he had painted, he replaced the animal with a water spaniel, modeled on Robert Havell's dog, Foxy.*

Robert Havell, Audubon's principal engraver, showed English Pheasants Surprised by a Dog *to the British portraitist, Sir Thomas Lawrence. Audubon recorded the esteemed artist's reaction to his work in his journal entry for December 26, 1828: "He approached it, looked at it sideways, up and down, and put his face close to the canvas, had it moved from one situation to two others in different lights, but gave no opinion." (Journals, 1:341–342)*

The Entrapped Otter (Canada Otter)

c. 1827–1830. Oil on fabric, 24⅛ × 29½".
Milwaukee Art Museum, Wisconsin. Purchase,
Layton Art Collection.

Audubon completed about fifty oil paintings during his life, and the otter ensnared in a trap was one of his favorite subjects, to which he returned often. While this copy was probably painted in 1827–1830, Audubon is known to have made an earlier version in England in 1826 as a gift for Mrs. Richard Rathbone, the wife of one of his most loyal supporters and patrons. Although Mrs. Rathbone intensely disliked the subject, her husband accepted it on her behalf. Audubon's journals record his intentions to paint additional copies for other friends he had acquired during his stay in England.

Audubon later painted the otter for inclusion in his publication on quadrupeds, in which he described the method of trapping these animals. "This species," he wrote of the otter, "has a singular habit of sliding off the wet sloping banks into the water, and the trappers take advantage of this habit to catch the animal by placing a steel-trap near the bottom of their sliding places, so that the Otters occasionally put their foot into it as they are swiftly gliding toward the water." (Quadrupeds, 2:7)

ENTREPRENEUR AND WRITER

Joseph Bartholomew Kidd
(1808–1889), after John James
Audubon. *Pileated Woodpecker*

1831. Oil on canvas, 25⅞ × 38⅜".
Courtesy, Department of Library Services,
American Museum of Natural History, New York.

*This oil copy of Audubon's watercolor
painting of the* Pileated Woodpecker
*was made in 1831 as part of a commission by Audubon to Joseph B. Kidd to copy
one hundred of his bird watercolors. The
existence of many of these copies still
causes confusion as to which oil paintings
are truly by Audubon. While over one
hundred oil paintings are attributed to
Audubon today, he painted only about
fifty during his lifetime.*

John James Audubon. *John James Audubon*

1826. Pencil and charcoal on paper, 5⅝ × 4¼".
Mr. Richard R. Rathbone, Green Bank, Liverpool,
England.

In this self-portrait, inscribed Audubon
at Green Bank/ Almost, Happy!!—/
Sepr 1826, *the artist has depicted himself
as a romantic figure, showing off his distinctive nose and flowing curly locks of
hair, the features of his own appearance
that pleased him the most.*

*The drawing, made for Mrs. William
Rathbone as a token of friendship,
expresses the pleasure Audubon felt in visiting her and her family at Green Bank,
their country estate near Liverpool, during
his extended visit to England in 1826 to
1829. Suffering from homesickness for his
family as well as for the forests and birds of
America, Audubon found solace in the
warm embrace of the Rathbones, away
from the social demands and pollution of
England's cities. "At five this morning I
left Manchester and its smoke behind me,"
Audubon wrote on September 28, 1826.
"The ride was a wet one, heavy rain
falling continuously. I was warmly welcomed by my good Liverpool friends, and
though completely drenched I felt it not, so
glad was I to be in Liverpool again. . . .
From here to Green Bank, where I am lit-
erally at home." (*Journals, 1:127) The
Rathbone family, including Mrs. William
Rathbone, Sr., her sons, William and
Richard Rathbone, and their wives, were
unfailingly helpful to Audubon in prepar-
ing a prospectus for* The Birds of America *publication and procuring subscribers
to the work.*

plate and print Audubon's drawings of birds. When the drawings were first placed before Lizars, by an artist trembling with anxiety, the engraver rose from his seat and exclaimed with astonishment and delight: "My God! I never saw anything like this before."[49]

Audubon took special care to bring examples of the larger birds—the Wild Turkey cock, the Wild Turkey hen and the Whooping Crane—to convince the engraver of the necessity of employing unusually large-sized paper to accommodate his life-sized representations of the birds. Lizars agreed to use the "double elephant" size of paper (about 39½ by 29½ inches), a decision which substantially increased the expense of the project. The original folio of *The Birds of America* became known as the Double Elephant Folio, reflecting the size of the paper. Though the paper was consistent throughout the folio, the size of the image printed on it varied. The Double Elephant Folio contained 435 plates and its original cost was $1,000 in the United States and £182 in England. The prints were issued in sets of five, reaching a total of eighty-seven sets.[50] Each set or "number" was to include one large plate, one medium, and three small, and as Audubon wrote, "the wild Turkey-cock is to be the large bird of my first number [set], to prove the necessity of the size of the work."[51] The large birds filled the entire sheet and the small birds were centered on the page with wide, blank margins around them.

Lizars was responsible for the first ten plates or two numbers from which prints were pulled for the folio. A work strike by the colorists in Lizar's studio (the engravings were printed in black and white and then hand colored), among other difficulties, propelled Audubon to seek out the famed Havell engraving firm of London. In a letter of August 6, 1827 to his wife Lucy, Audubon reported that "London affords all sorts of facilities imaginable or necessary for the Publication of such immense work and hereafter my *Principal* business will be carried on here—I have made arrangements with a Mr. Havell, an excellent Engraver who has a good establishment containing Printers—Colorers and Engravers So that I can have all under my eye. . . ."[52] The project was entrusted to Robert Havell, Jr. (1793–1878) in June, 1827, and he finished the job in the same month of 1838.

During this twelve-year collaboration, Audubon and Robert Havell, an artist in his own right, established a close relationship in spite of some predictable lapses. A silver loving cup marking the publication of the second volume of *The Birds of America* and bearing the inscription "To Robert Havell from his Friend John James Audubon 1834" is testimony to that friendship (p. 81). At the start of their collaboration Havell offered Audubon two advantages over Lizars: a production price that was significantly lower, and the addition of his skills as an aquatintist to the more established techniques of line engraving and etching. The aquatint process involves applying a resin ground to the copper plate which is heated, cooled, and etched. The ground provides for subtle variations in tone when the acid bites the image into the plate. Unlimited gradations from pale gray to velvety black and a pleasing granular effect characterize this form of etching. The finished aquatint impression includes the softer, intermediary shades of

John James Audubon's portable
lapdesk

Mahogany, folding.
Collection of The New-York Historical Society.

*The worn green felt surface of this folding
desk suggests the frequent use that Audubon made of it.*

ENTREPRENEUR AND WRITER

John James Audubon's beaded purse

Collection of The New-York Historical Society.

Lucy, Audubon's wife, made this beaded needlepoint purse, which served the artist well from 1826 to 1828 during his visit to England, where he socialized with wealthy friends and followed the custom of tipping their servants.

Common Loon

Audubon's name: Great Northern Diver or Loon.
1830. Robert Havell, engraver.
Copperplate, 41½ × 28½".
Courtesy, Department of Library Services,
American Museum of Natural History, New York.

This copperplate of the Common Loon, *as well as the uncolored engraving shown opposite, were intermediate steps in the creation of the final, colored engraving for the* Birds of America. *The copperplates were shipped over to America from England in 1839 at Audubon's request. Some were probably destroyed while in storage in New York City in the great fire of 1845, but most were salvaged and then stored by the Audubon family at Minnie's Land, the family estate on the Hudson River. In 1871, to raise money, the remaining plates were sold for scrap by Audubon's widow, Lucy, after a futile attempt to interest museums and collectors in their purchase. In 1873, the plates were in the process of being melted down when the alert fourteen-year-old son of the company's general manager noticed them and the surviving plates were removed to temporary safety. The boy's mother, interested by his account of the copperplates, visited the company during its annual inventory the following year and identified the works as Audubon's. At that point, the plates were deemed too important for destruction, and the company instead restored them by removing oxidation from their surfaces. About seventy-eight plates have been identified as extant, though some are not currently located. Most are in the collections of museums and universities, including The Metropolitan Museum of Art, The New-York Historical Society, the American Museum of Natural History in New York City, The Smithsonian Institution, Princeton University, and Yale University.*

Common Loon

Audubon's name: Great Northern Diver or Loon.
1830. Robert Havell, engraver.
Uncolored engraving, 41½ × 28¾".
Courtesy, Department of Library Services,
American Museum of Natural History, New York.

Audubon, in July of 1833 in Labrador, noted that his son John and Thomas Lincoln, a companion, "saw several Loons and tolled *them by running towards them hallooing and waving a handkerchief, at which sight and cry the loon immediately swam towards them, until within twenty yards. This 'tolling' is curious and wonderful. Many other species of waterfowl are deceived by these manoeuvres, but none so completely as the loon."* (Journals, *1:389) In subsequent journal entries during the Labrador trip, Audubon recorded his efforts to complete a drawing of the loon. On July 9 he notes, "I have drawn all day at the Loon, a most difficult bird to imitate." On July 10, he writes, "I tried to finish my drawing of the Loon, but in vain; I covered my paper to protect it from the rain, with the exception only of the few inches where I wished to work, and yet that small space was not spared by the drops that fell from the rigging on my table."* (Journals, *1:392,394) The completed drawing became the bird, in breeding plumage, on the right in the Havell print.*

Audubon considered these birds to be miracles of nature worthy of the closest scrutiny. "View it as it buoyantly swims over the heaving billows of the Atlantic, or as it glides along deeply immersed, when apprehensive of danger, on the placid lake, on the grassy islet of which its nest is placed," he recommended. "Calculate, if you can, the speed of its flight, as it shoots across the sky; mark the many plunges it performs in quest of its finny food, or in eluding its enemies; list to the loud and plaintive notes which it issues . . . and you will not count your labour lost, for you will have watched the ways of one of the wondrous creations of unlimited Power and unerring Wisdom." (Ornithological Biography, *4:43)*

gray, allowing for a closer approximation of the original watercolor medium.

Audubon was delighted with the quality of Havell's engravings (p. 79). The coloring of the plates, which was accomplished by the hands of dozens of people, did not always satisfy Audubon, as it had not when he worked with Lizars, so the artist monitored the production process carefully. On August 9, 1828, Audubon reported that his London days were exceptionally busy and included "journeys (often several times a day) to Havell's."[53]

Royal patronage was to provide an important stamp of approval, as well as financial support for the publication. Audubon sought an audience with George IV during his 1827 London stay, and although he was not successful in meeting with the king, he did eventually gather the promise of a subscription and the right to claim royal patronage for *The Birds of America*. King Charles X of France, who was to be deposed during the July 1830 Revolution, and the Duke of Orleans—who later, as King Louis Philippe, would reign until 1848—subscribed to the folio edition by this artist of French heritage. It was the French flower painter Pierre Joseph Redouté (1759–1840) who introduced Audubon to the Duke on September 20, 1828. When the artist held up the plate of the Northern (Baltimore) Oriole for the Duke's inspection, the future king said: "This surpasses all I have seen, and I am not astonished now at the eulogiums of M. Redouté."[54] Unfortunately, none of these royal patrons undertook to subsidize the entire project and thus relieve Audubon of the need for relentless promotion and sales.

American subscribers to the Double Elephant Folio edition included such prestigious institutions as the Library of Congress (which would have required two free copies if Audubon had published his work in the United States), the State Department, the Boston Athenaeum, Columbia College, and the American Philosophical Society. Prominent citizens, merchants, collectors, and naturalists fill the list of American subscribers to the first edition of the *Birds of America:* the Honorable Daniel Webster, Boston; Robert Gilmor, Esquire, Baltimore; Henry Clay, Jr., Esquire, Ashland, Kentucky.[55] The New York art patron Luman Reed, who formed a distinguished collection of European and contemporary American art during the 1830s, bought Audubon's work for his library. A generous and benevolent patron of Thomas Cole and Asher B. Durand, among other aspiring artists, Reed paid in advance for his copy of the third volume of the folio. "Such an unexpected favor at a moment, I acknowledge, I felt particularly the expenses attending my publication," wrote Audubon in a letter to Reed on January 7, 1835, "I shall ever think of with the deepest gratitude."[56] Unfortunately, Luman Reed died in 1836 before the publication of the fourth volume of the *Birds* and therefore was unable to complete the set. His was one of many incomplete subscriptions. During the almost twelve-year period that it took to publish the four volumes, some subscribers died, some faced economic difficulties, and others may have lost interest. Dropouts had to be replaced in order to make the publication profitable, so Audubon and his family continued to solicit subscribers on both sides of the Atlantic for many years. Audubon aimed to produce two hundred sets and, although it is not known how many sets were completed, it is

Loving Cup

1834. Silver. Height: 4½″, diameter: 3¾″.
John James Audubon State Park, Henderson,
Kentucky.

*Among the rich assortment of Audubon
family memorabilia and art at the John
James Audubon Memorial Museum in
Henderson, Kentucky, is this silver loving
cup inscribed* To Robert Havell from
his Friend John James Audubon,
1834. *The presentation marked the publication of the second volume of* The Birds
of America *and Audubon's gratitude for
the fine engraving of his principal collaborator in this multivolume work.*

thought that he almost met his goal.[57]

Audubon vigorously claimed that he was an inadequate writer, who could scarcely construct a tolerable sentence in French, much less English. He alleged that he would prefer to travel through the Florida swamps without a shirt during mosquito time than to put pen to paper. Nevertheless, he produced a prodigious amount of writing about nature. He was an active journal and letter writer and ultimately turned his many field notes into published volumes on natural history. He was compelled to publish his writings partly in order to confirm his stature as a naturalist. Early reviews of his plates considered them principally as works of art rather than science. Even his friend the English ornithologist William Swainson chose to speak of him "particularly as a painter," whose work should be judged "by the rules which constitute pictorial criticism."[58] Published writings, Audubon knew, would further his reputation as a scientific observer of nature and allow him to join the ranks of distinguished artist/recorders of the New World, some of whom served as inspirations to his own endeavor.

It is not known to what extent Audubon was familiar with the earliest European renderings of American wildlife. Some of these date from the sixteenth century when Portuguese, Spanish, English, and French explorers scanned the coastal areas, made maps of the terrain, and recorded populations of men, birds, beasts, and plants. Important visual and narrative records were produced by John White, an artist, and Thomas Hariot, a mapmaker, both of whom accompanied Walter Raleigh's expedition to Roanoke, Virginia, in 1585. White's drawings, which picture Native Americans engaged in customary activities and document impressive wildlife specimens, provide one of the few views of the wilderness as it existed before European settlement. White's drawings were engraved by Theodore de Bry and published in *America* (1588), accompanied by text from Thomas Hariot's *Briefe and true report on the new found land of Virginia*, which spread the enthusiasm for the rich and exotic landscape of the New World to a broader European audience (p. 89).

Between 1731 and 1743, Mark Catesby, a successor to White, traveled through America and produced the first extensive portrayal of flora and fauna in two volumes entitled the *Natural History of Carolina, Florida and the Bahama Islands*, a work well-known to Audubon. In his preface to the work, Catesby expressed an approach to natural history subjects that could well have served as a model for Audubon. "In designing the Plants, I always did them while fresh and just gather'd," wrote Catesby. "And the Animals, particularly the Birds, I painted them while alive (except a very few) and gave them their gestures peculiar to every kind of Bird, and where it would admit of, I have adapted the Birds to those Plants on which they fed, or have any relation to."[59] Catesby taught himself painting and engraving to produce his work and emphasized the legibility of his flat, unmodeled style which is reflected in his elegant profile representation of the *White Ibis* silhouetted against the contours of a leaf (p. 86). "Things done in Flat, tho' exact manner," suggested Catesby, "may serve the Purpose of Natural History, better in some Measure than in a more bold Painterlike Way."[60]

That Audubon disagreed with this aspect of Catesby's approach is demon-

Pileated woodpecker

Audubon's name: Pileated Woodpecker. 1829.
Robert Havell, engraver.
Hand-colored etching and aquatint, 23⅝ × 18¾".
Collection of The New-York Historical Society.

"So attached is this Woodpecker to the tree in which it has a hole," Audubon noted of the species he observed in Texas and on his Missouri River trip, *"that during winter it is often seen with its head out, as if looking to the weather, the unfavourable state of which induces it to sink out of sight, and probably compose itself to rest."* (Ornithological Biography, 5:333) In this image, two young males are shown quarreling on the lower branch. Above them are an adult male and, at the top, an adult female.

strated in both his drawing and his writings. Through close observation of birds engaged in activities particular to them, he preferred to capture the "characteristical manners" of each species of bird, and therefore avoided strictly profile views. He observed that among water birds, herons walked with an elegance and stateliness, and he represented this active, dignified posture in his drawing of the *Great Blue Heron* (p. 87). Furthermore he felt that a natural history painter should not adopt a style of flat forms circumscribed by clear contours to enhance the documentary clarity of specimen drawings. Instead, it was Audubon's contention that, like master artists since the Renaissance, the scientific artist should breathe life into the natural forms by employing the full range of compositional, spatial, and tonal techniques. "Among the naturalists of the time, several who are distinguished have said that representations of subjects ought to be entirely devoid of shades in all their parts; that the colouring of the figure, that must be precisely profile, cannot be understood by the student if differently represented," wrote Audubon derisively. "My opinion is, that he who cannot conceive and determine the *natural* colouring of a shaded part, need not study either natural history or any thing else connected with it."[61]

Another source of inspiration to Audubon in publishing his writings was William Bartram's 1791 publication *Travels Through North and South Carolina, Georgia, East and West Florida, The Cherokee Country, The Extensive Territories of the Muscogulges, or Creek Confederacy, and the Country of the Chactaws*, which he read prior to his travels to the southern states during the early 1830s. The son of John Bartram, who created the first botanical garden in America, William (1739–1823) grew up in a scientific household with a substantial natural history library at his disposal. In his youth, he accompanied his father on an expedition to collect and classify exotic specimens of flora and fauna in Florida. On behalf of the British botanist, John Fothergill, William set out independently, in 1773, on an exploration of the southeastern region. During a four-year journey seeking the "rare and useful productions of nature, chiefly the vegetable kingdom," he sent his patron botanical drawings, specimens, notes, and seeds. The 1791 publication of his *Travels*, developed from journal notes made during the trip, met with immediate success and was translated into several languages. A combined literary and scientific triumph, the book presented a poetic vision of the wilderness and paired it with literate descriptions of its particulars. It became a standard of excellence against which subsequent "roving nature reporters" such as Alexander Wilson and Audubon would measure their achievements.

As early as November, 1826, Audubon conceived of publishing a written work as a companion to his engraved illustrations of *The Birds of America*. The letterpress volume, which ultimately became five volumes entitled *Ornithological Biography, or an Account of the Habits of the Birds of the United States of America; Accompanied by Descriptions of the Objects Represented in the Work Entitled The Birds of America, and Interspersed with Delineations of American Scenery and Manners*, would contain descriptions of the birds and their habits drawn from his observations in the field as well as sixty informal essays based upon Audubon's frontier experiences from 1814–1834 and, perhaps, modeled upon the informal prose style of

John James Audubon. *Self-Portrait (in frontier garb for an English admirer)*

1826. Pencil on paper.
Courtesy, Mrs. Abraham Dixon, London.

Recognizing the English fascination with America as wilderness, and indulging his self-image as an American woodsman, Audubon sketched this self-portrait in frontier garb for one of his admirers during his visit to England in 1826. "I cannot help expressing my surprise," he wrote in his journal in 1826, "that the people of England, generally speaking, are so unacquainted with the customs and localities of our country. The principal conversation about it always turns to Indians and their ways, as if the land produced nothing else." (Journals, 1:120)

George Caleb Bingham. *Daniel Boone Escorting Settlers Through the Cumberland Gap*

1851–52. Oil on canvas, 36½ × 50¼".
Washington University Gallery of Art, St. Louis.

Mark Catesby (1682/3–1749).
White Ibis

Catesby's name: White Curlew. c. 1727–31.
Hand-colored etching, 13¾ × 10¼".
New York Public Library.

When Mark Catesby published Natural
History of Carolina, Florida, and the
Bahama Islands, *between 1731 and
1743, the two-volume set of prints and
written descriptions represented the first
extensive portrayal of the plant and animal life of America. While the majority of
plates depicted birds, Catesby also painted
small mammals, insects, and marine animals. A native Englishman, Catesby studied and painted the subjects of his art
during two extended visits to America—
the first in Virginia from 1712 to 1719,
and the second in the Carolinas, Georgia,
Florida, and the Bahamas from 1722 to
1726. Upon his return to England in
1726, Catesby learned to etch so that he
could personally engrave the plates in his*
Natural History, *including twenty in
the Appendix added in 1747. For the first
edition of his work, he also colored the
plates by hand himself, or personally
supervised the process.*

In this etching of The White Ibis,
*Catesby has set the bird against the back-
ground of a golden club leaf, in keeping
with his method of joining plants and animals of a locale in a single plate in pro-
portional scale. Although presented simply
in profile, the White Ibis retains the image
of vibrancy for which Catesby's art is
known.*

Great Blue Heron

Audubon's name: Great Blue Heron. 1821 and 1834. Pastel, watercolor, graphite, oil, gouache, and collage on paper, 36 × 25⅜″.
Collection of The New-York Historical Society.

"Few of our waders are more interesting than the [Great Blue Heron]," wrote Audubon. "Their contours and movements are always graceful, if not elegant. Look on the one that stands near the margin of the pure stream:—see his reflection dipping as it were into the smooth water. . . . How calm, how silent, how grand is the scene!" (Ornithological Biography, 3:87) *Audubon observed this large wading bird which can be found from Canada to Mexico on Jestico Island (on his trip to Labrador) and on the St. John's River in East Florida.*

Audubon noted that the Great Blue Heron eats all kinds of fish, but it also has more exotic tastes, devouring "frogs, lizards, snakes, and birds, as well as small quadrupeds, such as shrews, meadow-mice, and young rats, all of which I have found in its stomach. Aquatic insects are equally welcome to it, and it is an expert flycatcher, striking at moths, butterflies, and libellulae, whether on the wing or when alighted." (Ornithological Biography, 3:92)

Bartram's *Travels.* Audubon began writing the *Ornithological Biography* in 1830; the last volume was published in 1839. The technical descriptions, for which Audubon enlisted the editorial services of the Scottish ornithologist William MacGillivray (1796–1852), aimed to satisfy a scholarly audience with the seriousness of the author's scientific purpose. The essays, or "Episodes," which were sprinkled through the first three volumes of the *Ornithological Biography* were designed to relieve the tedium of the nearly five hundred life histories of birds, to express his personal frontier experience, and to attract a wider audience. Based upon his nature travels from 1818–1834, the Episodes satisfied a desire on the part of his readers for a secondhand wilderness experience through an authentic voice. "If Mr. Audubon had contented himself with Linnaean descriptions," wrote an admiring critic, "he would have had the honor of discovering more birds than readers."[62]

In his writing as much as in his drawing, Audubon emphasized a truth or authenticity based upon direct experience. He perceived himself as a privileged witness to the secrets of an untouched wilderness and a passing culture of frontier life. This role filled him with a sense of wonder and awe. He viewed the disappearance of the wilderness and the development of civilization with a clear eye, but he resisted passing strong moral judgment. "Whether these changes are for the better or for the worse," Audubon mused in uncharacteristically modest fashion, "I shall not pretend to say."[63] He did firmly believe that "the original state of the country" needed to be preserved in writing before it was too late. He felt that the task ultimately should be accomplished by the best writers of the period, namely Washington Irving and James Fenimore Cooper. In the meantime, the Episodes offered his written record of the contours and customs of this fast-disappearing, unsettled land.

When I think of these times, and call back to my mind the grandeur and beauty of those almost uninhabited shores; when I picture to myself the dense and lofty summits of the forest, that everywhere spread along the hills, and overhung the margins of the stream, unmolested by the axe of the settler; when I know how dearly purchased the safe navigation of that river has been by the blood of many worthy Virginians; when I see that no longer any Aborigines are to be found there, and that vast herds of elks, deer and buffaloes which once pastured on these hills and in these valleys, making for themselves great roads to the several salt-springs, have ceased to exist; when I reflect that all this grand portion of our Union, instead of being in a state of nature, is now more or less covered with villages, farms, and towns, where the din of hammers and machinery is constantly heard; that the woods are fast disappearing under the axe by day, and the fire by night; hundreds of steam-boats are gliding to and fro, over the whole length of the majestic river, forcing commerce to take root and to prosper at every spot; when I see the surplus population of Europe coming to assist in the destruction of the forest, and transplanting civilization into its darkest recesses;—when I remember that these extraordinary changes have all taken place in the short period of twenty years, I pause, wonder, and, although I know all to be fact, can scarcely believe its reality.[64]

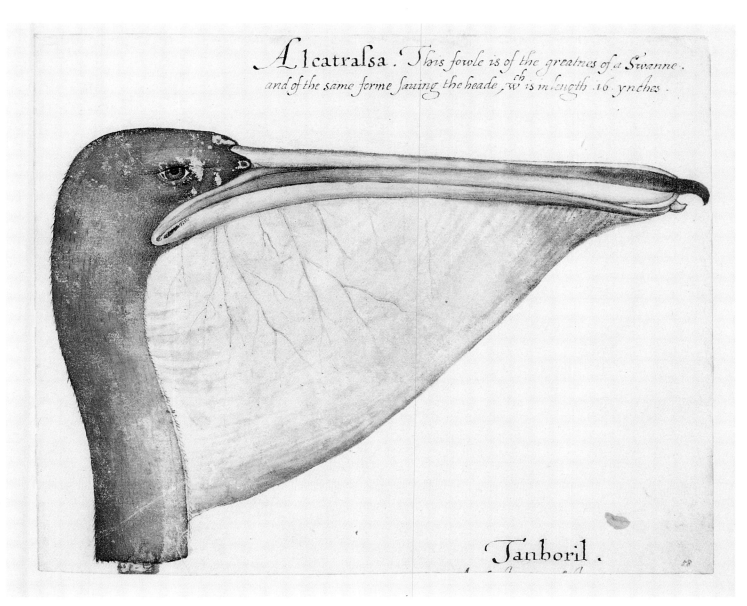

*Alcatralsa. This fowle is of the greatnes of a Swanne.
and of the same forme sauing the heade, wth is in length .16. ynches.*

Tanboril.

John White (b. 1540). *Head of a
Brown Pelican*

1585–1593. Watercolor over graphite, heightened
with white, on paper, 7¼ × 8¾″.
The British Museum, London.

*This depiction of the head of the Eastern
Brown Pelican, a species not seen in England, represents the work of the British
artist-naturalist, John White. Among the
earliest extant images of New World
wildlife, White's sixteenth-century drawings were made during an exploratory trip
led by Sir Walter Raleigh. The word "Tanboril" at the bottom of the page refers to a
drawing of a puffer fish that was separated from this sheet.*

John White (b. 1540). *Flamingo*

1585–1593. Watercolor over graphite, touched with white (oxydized), 11⅜ × 7¾".
The British Museum, London.

Little is known about John White, the official artist of the British expedition to Virginia in 1585 and governor of the colony there in 1587. He did, however, leave behind many maps of the New World and drawings of its wildlife and inhabitants. As his elegant Flamingo *drawing shows, White combined in his art a delicate use of the brush with precision of line and dense coloration. Since White never visited Florida, where the Greater Flamingo may be found, this painting may be a copy of a work by another artist.*

Drawn from Nature by J.J. Audubon, F.R.S. F.L.S.   *Purple Grakle or Common Crow Blackbird.*   Engraved by W.H. Lizars Edin.ᵣ
QUISCALUS VERSICOLOR, *Vieill.* Male 1. Female 2.   Maize or Indian Corn Zea Mays.   Retouched by R. Havell Jun.ʳ London 1831.

Common Grackle

Audubon's name: Purple Grackle. 1825. Robert
Havell, engraver.
Hand-colored etching and aquatint, 26½ × 20¾".
New York Public Library.

Audubon describes his image of the Common Grackle, a large blackbird with iridescent plumage, precisely. "Look at them," he exhorted. "The male, as if full of delight at the sight of the havoc which he has already committed on the tender, juicy, unripe corn on which he stands, has swelled his throat, and is calling in exultation to his companions to come and assist in demolishing it. The female has fed herself, and is about to fly off with a well-loaded bill to her hungry and expectant brood, that from the nest, look on their plundering parents. . . . See how the husk is torn from the ear, and how nearly devoured are the grains of corn! This is the tithe our Blackbirds take from our planters and farmers; but it was so appointed, and such is the will of the beneficent Creator." (Ornithological Biography, *1:35*)

Although Audubon decries the "nefarious propensities" of the grackle, he admires the deep and various tints of its feathers. "The genial rays of the sun shine on their silky plumage, and offer to the ploughman's eye such rich and varying tints, that no painter, however gifted, could ever imitate them. The coppery bronze, which in one light shows its rich gloss, is, by the least motion of the bird, changed in a moment to brilliant and deep azure, and again, in the next light, becomes refulgent sapphire or emerald green." (Ornithological Biography, *1:35*) Audubon *knew this bird as the "Purple Grackle," which was formerly considered a separate species from the "Bronze Grackle." Today, the different types are regarded as two varieties of the same species, the Common Grackle, which is found throughout the eastern United States and Canada.*

Like the self-portrait of himself suspended over a chasm in his painting of the *Golden Eagle*, Audubon projected himself as an heroic protagonist in his written rendition of frontier life (p. 85, top). Whether he was recording such dramatic natural disasters as earthquakes or floods, or instructing his reader on how to butcher a buffalo or locate a turtle egg, he inserted himself into the center of the scene, whether he was actually there or not. The authenticity of the tale derived from the strength and grandeur of his frontier persona. He claimed that his sole inspiration was the desire to gain knowledge and pass it along. This knowledge was drawn from his written notes, his memory, and from tales that were told to him. As he traveled along the river, hunted in the woods, or sat around the campfire, he gathered local stories and retold them as his own.

One Episode recounts an adventure that was supposed to have occurred some twenty years earlier when Audubon was traveling with his frontier hero, Daniel Boone (see p. 85, bottom). After returning from a hunting expedition together, during which Boone had displayed extraordinary skill with his rifle, the two men bedded down for the night. Both preferred to sleep on blankets on the floor instead of on the soft beds nearby. Boone proceeded to tell a famous story of his being captured by Indians in Kentucky and how he ingeniously escaped by getting the squaws drunk. The story was a well known frontier myth by the time Audubon told it, but it took on immediate authenticity because the artist claimed to have heard it firsthand.

Audubon probably never met Boone, but his larger-than-life picture of the man clearly rings true as an alter ego for himself. "The stature and general appearance of this wanderer of the western forests approached the gigantic. His chest was broad and prominent; his muscular powers displayed themselves in every limb," wrote Audubon of Boone's appearance. "His countenance gave indication of his great courage, enterprise, and perseverance; and when he spoke, the very motion of his lips brought the impression that whatever he uttered could not be otherwise that strictly true."[65] The two men shared a devotion to the wilderness, lofty ambition, impressive demeanors, and a dedication to tall tales and truthful appearances.

Mark Catesby (1682/3–1749).
Flamingo

Hand-colored etching, 14 × 10¼".
New York Public Library.

Mark Catesby's hand-colored etching of the Flamingo, *completed between 1727 and 1731 for inclusion in the first volume of his* Natural History of Carolina, Florida, and the Bahama Islands, *shows the artist's characteristic simplicity and compositional talent. The bird's placement against the small, stylized tree both reveals the flamingo's size and lends a decorative background to the long, narrow figure. In addition, Catesby departed from the traditional scientific method of presenting wildlife specimens out of context on a blank page by portraying the Flamingo in a landscape environment.*

IV. Western Travels; The Viviparous Quadrupeds of North America

Roseate Spoonbill

Audubon's name: Roseate Spoonbill. c. 1831–1832, in Florida.
Watercolor, graphite, selective glazing, and gouache on paper, 23⅛ × 35¹¹/₁₆".
Collection of The New-York Historical Society.

"The sight of a flock of fifteen or twenty of these full-dressed birds is extremely pleasing to the student of nature," Audubon wrote of the Roseate Spoonbill. *"They all stand with their wings widely extended to receive the sun's rays, or perhaps to court the cooling breeze. . . . They all stalk about with graceful steps along the margin of the muddy pool, or wade in the shallows in search of food."* (Ornithological Biography, 4:189) *Audubon observed the birds in Texas and south Florida, where they are "found for the most part along the marshy and muddy borders of estuaries, the mouths of rivers, ponds, or sea islands or keys partially overgrown with bushes, and perhaps still more commonly along the shores of those singular salt-water bayous."* (Ornithological Biography, 4:188)

The beauty of the mature Roseate Spoonbill's pink and red feathers, sought after by milliners, brought it to the brink of extinction in the early twentieth century. It survives today under the protection of conservation laws. The young Spoonbills are born almost entirely white and develop their distinctive color within three years. A wading bird, the Roseate Spoonbill feeds by sweeping its broad bill from side to side under water in search of small fish, crustaceans, and insects. The bird in this drawing is about to enter the water in such a pursuit. The background was probably painted—with notations to be followed by Robert Havell in completing the print—by George Lehman, Audubon's assistant and traveling companion to the Florida Keys in 1831 and 1832.

Primarily acting as his own agent, Audubon spent almost four years abroad, pursuing subscribers to his publication *The Birds of America*. Through exhibiting his original drawings at public institutions, private homes, and his own personal lodgings, he gathered recognition and clients to purchase subscriptions to the publication. By having oil copies of his bird drawings made for sale, and by producing new wildlife game pictures himself, Audubon made money to support himself and his project. His relentless work, travel, writing, painting, and exhibition schedule prompted him on more than one occasion to fear that his health would not hold up or, at least, to wish that he possessed more than two hands. Nevertheless, he recognized with satisfaction, shortly before his departure from London to New York in 1831, that in this entrepreneurial venture he had succeeded as he had not in the past. "I have balanced my accounts with *The Birds of America* and the whole business is really wonderful," he wrote with undisguised pleasure. "*Forty Thousand Dollars!* have passed through my hands for the completion of the first volume." He wondered, "Who would believe that a lonely individual, who landed in England without a friend in the whole country, and with only sufficient pecuniary means to travel it as a visitor, could have accomplished such a task as this publication?"[66]

Financially secure and with an established reputation gained abroad, Audubon wanted to return again to the woods of America. While still in Europe, he made plans to explore the peninsula of Florida, especially the Keys. He further hoped to cross the Mississippi River and the Rocky Mountains and document the birds and other wildlife of the western territories. The Florida plan was accomplished and did enlarge his publication with some of his most magnificent artistic productions. The western excursion did not materialize, at least under its original conception, due to a shortage of funds and the artist's failing health.

Audubon arrived in New York from London early in August, 1831, with his wife and a young English taxidermist, Henry Ward, whom he had hired to help with mounting specimens for his drawings and preserving skins to be gathered on the Florida expedition. On his route south, he made a stop in Philadelphia, where he engaged George Lehman (c.1800–1870), a landscape painter of Swiss descent, who would also accompany them. Lucy was dispatched to join her family in Louisville, Kentucky, while the artist and his companions gained passage aboard a government revenue cutter which would sail from Washington, D.C., south along the coast. During a stop in Charleston, South Carolina, Audubon made the fortuitous acquaintance of the Reverend John Bachman, a Lutheran

minister with a passion for nature that matched his own. "I had passed by one night in the city, when I was presented to the Rev. Mr. Bachman," Audubon reported. "This benevolent man, whom I am proud to call my friend, would not suffer the 'American Woodsman' to repose any where but under his roof; and not him alone—all his assistants too."[67] Bachman served as host to the whole party during their monthlong stay in the city and guided them on specimen excursions in the surrounding countryside. Audubon formed a strong personal and professional bond with Bachman, who would later co-author Audubon's last multivolume publication, *The Viviparous Quadrupeds of North America* (1845–1848). Bachman's sister-in-law, Maria Martin (1796–1863), developed her already established flower painting skills under Audubon's guidance to a level of accomplishment that persuaded him to use her as a collaborator on some of his later drawings. The familial connection was further cemented by the marriage of Audubon's two sons, John and Victor, to two of Bachman's daughters, Maria and Eliza.

Audubon and his companions were anxious to catch the bird migrations south, and they did arrive in St. Augustine, Florida, in November, 1831. The magnificent water birds of these regions were the principal object of Audubon's excursion and he set out immediately to capture on paper their graceful forms and brilliant plumage. In his unfinished original drawing of the *Roseate Spoonbill* (p. 95), Audubon poses this large member of the Ibis family on a muddy bank, shifting its weight from its back leg to its front leg and spreading its wings as it advances toward the water. There it will feed on the small fish, aquatic insects, and mollusks with the distinctive spoon-shaped bill that gives the bird its name. George Lehman used watercolor to provide the grassy enclosure for the bird and penciled in a distant background setting in a diminutive scale to offset the grandeur of the Spoonbill, which dominates three-quarters of the page.

Audubon observed and reproduced the bird following its spring molt in March when its plumage is at the peak of its beauty. In meticulous detail, he represented the extraordinary color, texture, pattern, and shape of the bird's head, neck and bill, recording the subtle color modulations on the various surface textures of this remarkable bird in watercolor and gouache. From the tip of its hard gray bill, through its wrinkled green head and soft pink plumage, to its yellowish tail feathers, the artist has captured and enhanced the palette of his subject. Audubon gives weight and volume to his colorful production by opening up the bird's rosy-tinted wings, which cast a deep shadow and thereby emphasize the roundness of its underbody. The outspread wings convey a vigorous impression of the bird's active advance to the water and, like ailerons, balance its weight on the approach. This is clearly no dried specimen, but a bird depicted in the full flush of life and action.

The artist incised patterns of various geometries into the bill, the skin, the feathers, and the legs of the Spoonbill. Lines in the shape of beehive scales cover the bird's legs and feet like netting, while irregular configurations appear and disappear on the bird's bill. Within this extravagant visual display of color and pattern, the artist maintains a center of focus. The brilliant glassy pink eye of the

Spoonbill, encased in the wrinkled green skin of its head like a jewel in a gift box, provides a commanding highlight to the composition and reasserts the vigor of the bird.

The *Great Egret* (p. 104) is another elegant water bird that Audubon first observed with care in the wild and depicted from shot and live specimens in Key West, Florida. In his almost fully finished original drawing, Audubon poses the bird on the mud flats at the water's edge amid a series of mud chimneys belonging to the crayfish, a favorite food of the Great Egret. Indeed, the bird takes an aggressive posture with its neck bent down and retracted in anticipation of lunging at its quarry. "While on these banks," Audubon noted, "they stand motionless, rarely moving toward their prey, but waiting until it comes near, when they strike it and swallow it alive, or when large beat it on the water, or shake it violently, biting it severely all the while."[68] In fact, the object of the egret's desire is not a crayfish but a horned toad that does not appear in this original drawing. It was plucked later by Robert Havell from Audubon's painting of *Swainson's Hawk* and inserted into the final engraving of the *Great Egret*.

While the S-shaped curve of the egret's head and neck is not an unnatural position for the bird, it did solve a technical problem for the artist. Audubon had determined to represent every bird in its natural size and such long-necked, five-foot-tall birds as this egret offered a challenge even to the largest elephant folio sheets. The graceful bend in the egret's neck served the double purpose of fitting the bird neatly into the confines of the paper and enhancing the visual design of the composition. It is certain that Audubon took great pains over the bird's head and neck for he replaced the one drawn on the sheet with a cut-out from another of his own drawings of the same bird and pasted it onto this composition. Such collage work played an important preparatory role in Audubon's working method. Cut-outs allowed him to make improvements to forms inaccurately rendered, to fill in background voids, or to adjust shapes to suit the goals of his design. These visible second thoughts on Audubon's original paintings provide fascinating insights into the artist's creative process. As he had with the Roseate Spoonbill, Audubon painted the Great Egret at the time of year when the bird looks its best. The fine evanescent feathers of its breeding plumage are traced, strand for strand, with paint brushes made of individual bristles prepared by the artist especially for the purpose. The gossamer threads of this thin, white overcoat are amplified against the deep greenish-blue aquatic setting provided, probably, by Lehman. Indeed, the monumental beauty of Audubon's representation of the bird matches the artist's perception in the wild. Concealed in the grasses of a Florida marsh, he watched a magnificent flock including Great Egrets alight on a neighboring key. "They stood perched like so many newly finished statues of the purest alabaster," he wrote with rapturous delight, "forming a fine contrast to the deep blue sky."[69]

Audubon's reverent and poetic descriptions of birds aptly convey how much he enjoyed the pursuit and capture of his prey. They belie, however, the hardships that the life of the active naturalist entailed. When he and his companions spent their days either seeking or drawing birds, they arose well before dawn and retired long after sundown. "If the day is to be spent at drawing, Lehman and I take a walk, and Ward, his gun, dog, and basket, returning when hungry or fatigued, or both. We draw uninterruptedly till dusk, after which another walk, then write up our journals."[70] If no specimens were on hand for drawing, the men cleaned their guns overnight and prepared a lunch of bread, cheese, whiskey and water in the morning and set out in a rowboat through the marshes before daybreak. After hours of rowing, they anchored the boat and waded "through mud and water, amid myriads of sand-flies and mosquitoes, shooting here and there a bird, or squatting down on our hams for half an hour to observe the ways of the beautiful beings we are in pursuit of."[71] In the evening, as the birds flew over them to their roosting places, the men observed their characteristics in flight. After that, they rowed their boat back to camp but not to sleep. If some of the species they had captured were to be drawn the next day, they were skinned and sketched that evening to capture the brilliancy of their plumage before it faded and "to save them from incipient putridity."[72] By nightfall, Audubon admitted, he and his companions were tired out from their labors. The fatigue brought on by the pursuit of birds in their natural habitat was a pleasant one for Audubon in comparison with the weariness he experienced from the rigors of marketing and publishing his work. The physical challenges and discomforts of the wilderness were necessary bumps along the road that Audubon traveled seeking a new truth of nature that could only, in his view, be gained from direct experience. It is nonsense ever to hope," he wrote with conviction, "to see in the closet what is only to be perceived—as far as the laws, arrangements and beauties of ornithological nature is concerned,—by that devotion of time, opportunities, and action, to which I have consecrated my life, not without hope that science may benefit by my labours."[73]

While many of Audubon's images of water birds represent the predator poised to capture its prey, he shows the *Great Blue Heron* (pp. 100 and 101) at the moment of triumph, erect with confidence, holding the fish aloft in the vise of its long, sharp bill. Audubon makes clear, however, that this was no easy victory. Still crouched in its fishing posture, the bird's mud-stained legs record the slogging effort required to achieve this goal.

Until very recently, the Great Blue Heron and the Great White Heron were considered to be separate species and Audubon shared that view, but now ornithologists categorize the Great White Heron as a color phase or subspecies of the Great Blue Heron. Its pure white and graceful form is set off to magnificent effect by the artist, who surrounds it with a cushion of deep blue sky. Beneath the bird's body is a thin line of buildings representing the waterfront of Key West, where Audubon studied the bird in 1832.

Audubon's inscriptions on the original drawing (not shown here) indicate the firm control he exerted over the transfer of the image from the watercolor original to the engraved plate. His verbal instructions form a carpet over the sandy ground under the White Heron's feet. He indicates precise directions about color, from the grand scheme to the particular detail: "Keep closely to the Sky in depth and colouring; have the water of a Pea-green tint. keep the division of the scales on

1 Roseate Spoonbill.   2 American Avocet.   3 Ruddy Plover.   4 Semipalmated Sandpiper.

Alexander Wilson (1766–1813).
Roseate Spoonbill, American Avocet, Ruddy Plover, Semipalmated Sandpiper

c. 1811. Hand-colored etching, 8¾ × 5½".
New York Public Library. Alexander Wilson, *American Ornithology; or, The Natural History of the Birds of the United States* (London: Whittaker, Treacher, & Arnot, 1832), Vol. 3, Plate 63 (page 26).

Calling the Roseate Spoonbill a "stately and elegant bird that inhabits the seashores of America, from Brazil to Georgia," Alexander Wilson regretted that he had never had the opportunity of observing the species in the wild, wading about in quest of shellfish and marine insects. (Wilson, American Ornithology, 3:26). His image was based on a specimen of such good quality, however, that it subsequently entered the collection of the Peale Museum founded in Philadelphia in the 1780s by Charles Willson Peale.

Great Blue Heron

Audubon's name: Great White Heron. 1832.
Robert Havell, engraver.
Hand-colored etching and aquatint, 25¼ × 38⅝".
New York Public Library.

Audubon first observed these birds in the Florida Keys in the spring of *1832*. One night, he and his companions parked in boats from midnight to daybreak, waiting for the herons to leave their roosts in search of food. During his visit, he captured several alive to give as pets to his friend Reverend John Bachman in Charleston. Another he shot as a specimen on which to base his drawing.

Calling this the "largest species of the heron tribe hitherto found in the United States," Audubon noted that the bird was "remarkable not only for its great size, but also for the pure white of its plummage [sic] at every period of its life." The "Great White Heron" is, in fact, the largest white heron in North America. Today, however, despite its all-white plumage, it is considered a subspecies of the Great Blue Heron, which has a much broader range. This heron is found only in keys, salt bays, and mud flats of south Florida, Cuba, and coastal Yucatán.

In the drawing on which this print was based, Audubon depicted the heron moments after catching a fish. He had confidence in the accuracy of his direct observations of bird behavior, even when they contradicted current ornithological opinion. "Among the varied and contradictory descriptions of Herons, you will find it alleged that these birds seize fish while on wing by plunging the head and neck into the water; but this seems to me extremely doubtful. Nor, I believe, do they watch for their prey while perched on trees." (Ornithological Biography, *3:550*)

Great Blue Heron

Audubon's name: Great White Heron. 1835.
Robert Havell, engraver.
Uncolored engraving, 41½ × 28¾".
Courtesy, Department of Library Services,
American Museum of Natural History, New York.

This uncolored engraving of the Great Blue Heron, *along with the colored engraving, illustrates the interim stages in the four-step process of producing* The Birds of America. *The first step was the watercolor painting of the bird by Audubon. Next came the engraving of the copperplate, the first ten by William Lizars (1788–1859) in Edinburgh and the rest by Robert Havell, Jr. (1793–1878) in London. Havell, a master engraver, had refined the technique of aquatinting,* which involved sprinkling resin on the plate before it went into the acid bath, so that the acid would bite irregularly, creating a tonal effect true to the original watercolor. Third, the plate was printed, producing a black and white engraving such as the one shown here, and finally the engraving was colored by hand. While Audubon performed a dominant or exclusive role in only the first step of this process, he also closely supervised the interim and final stages of the print-making.*

the legs & feet white in your engraving," he wrote to Havell on the sheet. He wanted the houses of Key West finished in more precise detail, but he also required a "mellowing in the outline" of some portions of the bird's anatomy, thereby enhancing the contrast of soft animate form with the crisp contours of civilization.

It was not water birds alone that attracted Audubon to Key West. At Reverend Bachman's house in Charleston, Audubon had seen the head of a "pigeon" that intrigued him because he could not identify it. Knowing that it was a native of the Florida Keys, Audubon was keen to locate the bird during his stay in that region. After a particularly arduous search through mosquito-infested, dense thickets, Audubon caught his first glimpse of the *Key West Quail-Dove* (p. 112), which had just been shot down by his companion. "How I gazed on its resplendent plumage!—how I marked the expression of its rich-coloured, large and timid eye, as the poor creature was gasping its last breath!—Ah, how I looked on this lovely bird! I handled it, turned it, examined its feathers and form, its bill, its legs and claws, weighed it by estimate, and after a while formed a winding sheet for it of a piece of paper. Did ever an Egyptian pharmacopolist employ more care in embalming the most illustrious of the Pharaohs, than I did in trying to preserve from injury this most beautiful of the woodland cooers!"[74] In fact, the changing metallic hues of this bird's glorious plumage made Audubon doubt that any artist could reproduce the splendor of the original. However, with the help of a botanical setting provided by George Lehman, Audubon depicted this elegant pair of doves almost to his own satisfaction.

It was the American Flamingo, more than any other bird, that Audubon hoped to find and record from life with his brush on his trip to the Florida Keys. On May 7, 1832, Audubon and his companions witnessed, against a magical twilight sky, a flock of Flamingoes in flight, with necks and legs fully extended, sailing overhead several times, but escaping the report of the travelers' guns. Audubon observed carefully the "glowing tints" of this deep pink bird and its majestic form on several more outings in the Keys, but he had to rely on specimens sent to him in London from Cuba in 1838 to make his watercolor image. This must have been a great disappointment to an artist who "ascertained that *feathers* lose their brilliancy almost as rapidly as flesh or skin itself, and," he continued, "that a bird alive is 75 per cent more rich in colours than twenty-four hours after its death."[75] Audubon managed to keep the saturated pink of the live Flamingo daubed in his imagination until he put it to paper in *American Flamingo* (p. 113), some six years later.

He adopted a posture for the Flamingo similar to that of the *Great Egret*, with neck and head bent down in a gentle S-shaped curve that creates a visual counterpoint with the advancing legs and allows the life-sized image to fit on the page. In comparison to the upright posture of the *Flamingo* presented in a drawing by British artist John White (p. 90), made over two hundred years earlier, Audubon's bird looks surrealistically distorted, yet it does represent the posture of a Flamingo, a filter feeder, engaged in a stately advance to the water to capture its prey.

During the 1830s, Audubon's extensive travels included a sailing trip to

Labrador in the summer of 1833 (his last important exploratory trip for birds) and numerous Atlantic crossings. The pressure to complete *The Birds of America* for publication, coupled with those of arduous travel and writing, forced Audubon to modify his working methods. To save time, he occasionally purchased or borrowed skins from institutions or fellow naturalists, as he did in the case of the American Flamingo (p. 113). He cut out drawings of birds such as the *Roseate Tern* (p. 117) and pasted them on new backgrounds, and he integrated more than one species of bird onto a single sheet, some pilfered from earlier drawings. The lack of personal contact with the bird in the wild and the rushed working method sometimes compromised the quality of his work.

However, some of his most visually or dramatically arresting images emerged at the same time. Audubon had only a fleeting acquaintance with a live *Great Grey Owl* (p. 116), which he saw in the winter of 1832 flying over Boston harbor. He made his drawing a few years later from a specimen borrowed from the Zoological Society of London and descriptive notes by the naturalist John Richardson.[76] The compact outline of this monochromatic bird perched upon a simple branch and set against a pure white background creates an image of startling elegance. Within a very limited tonal range of browns and grays, the intricate patterns of the owl's plumage command close scrutiny. From the barred wings and tail feathers, to the speckled breast, to the spherical ripples of the facial discs, the plumage of the bird becomes a selective summary of natural design. So compelling was this concentrated image that it was transferred essentially unaltered from the original drawing to the finished plate and it has often been given pride of place in subsequent publications and exhibitions devoted to Audubon's work.

Audubon admired the *Common Goldeneye* (p. 108) particularly for its speed of flight. Perhaps the swiftest of waterfowl, this duck impressed Audubon for the whistling sound produced by the rapid beat of its wings as it arose quickly through the air to evade an aggressor. How ingenious, then, to depict a pair of the ducks at a moment of arrested flight. The male, at the left, has just been shot in the wing, which droops and has rotated its axis abruptly, projecting downward from the impact of the shell and the loss of balance. (In the original painting, blood drips from his beak, dramatizing his demise.) His female companion, startled and momentarily frozen, appears to grip the sky with her webbed feet to regain her equilibrium and momentum. Depicting the birds at a moment of crisis, when their foremost weapon for protection—rapidity of flight—has been blasted, Audubon reinforced the drama with the irregular, agitated contours of form produced by wings, legs, and tails spread out in disarray. Implied, but not represented, in the image is the hunter, whose shot has stunned these fast-moving ducks.

A work that begs comparison with Audubon's *Common Goldeneye* is an oil painting by Winslow Homer, in which a hunter does appear in the background.[77] Painted in 1909 and entitled *Right and Left* (p. 109), Homer's last painting shows a pair of the same species, similarly configured on the page. Also responding to reports from a shot gun, one Goldeneye is catapulted upside down and the other

Great Egret

Audubon's name: Great White Heron. 1832.
Watercolor, graphite, gouache, and collage on
paper, 24³⁄₁₆ × 35½".
Collection of The New-York Historical Society.

*In this painting of 1832, Audubon
depicts the Great Egret, a member of the
Heron family, with all the stately beauty he
admired in its plumage and its movements. "On foot its movements are as
graceful as those of the Louisiana Heron,
its steps measured, its long neck gracefully
retracted and curved, and its silky train
reminded one of the flowing robes of the
noble ladies of Europe." (*Ornithological
Biography, *4:601) It was the magnifi-
cence of the bird's train, which develops
prior to the mating season and deteriorates
after the incubation of the eggs, that
placed the egret in danger of disappearance. Audubon worried that, "the long*

*plumes of this bird being in request for
ornamental purposes, they are shot in
great numbers while sitting on their eggs,
or soon after the appearance of the young.
I know a person who, on offering a double-
barrelled gun to a gentleman near
Charleston, for one hundred White
Herons fresh killed, received that number
and more the next day." (*Ornithological
Biography, *4:603–604)*

*Fortunately, today the Great Egret is
protected by wildlife conservation laws
passed earlier in this century. It thrives on
the shores, marshes, and ponds of the east
coast of North and South America—in the
United States, from the mid-Atlantic
states, throughout Florida, and along the
coast of Texas.*

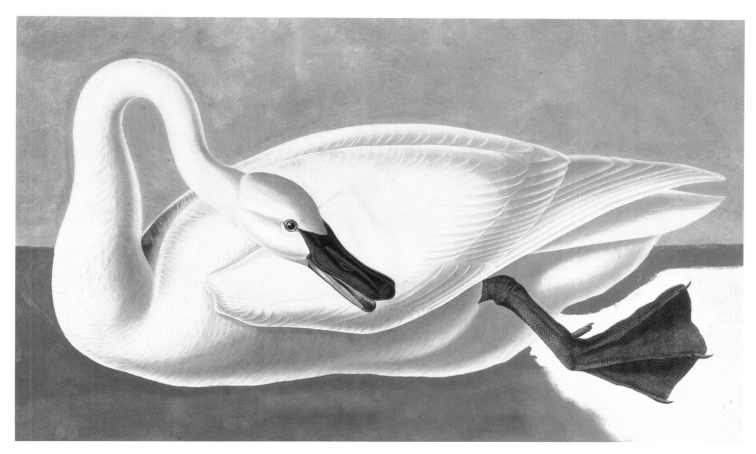

Trumpeter Swan

Audubon's name: Trumpeter Swan. Probably
c. 1836–1837.
Watercolor, pastel, oil, graphite, and selected
scraping on paper, 23 × 37¾".
Collection of The New-York Historical Society.

"To form a perfect conception of the beauty and elegance of these Swans," Audubon declared, *"you must observe them when they are not aware of your proximity, and as they glide over the waters of some secluded inland pond. On such occasions, the neck, which at other times is held stiffly upright, moves in graceful curves, now bent forward, now inclined backwards over the body. Now with an extended scooping movement the head becomes immersed for a moment, and with a sudden effort a flood of water is thrown over the back and wings, when it is seen rolling off in sparkling globules, like so many large pearls."* (Ornithological Biography, 4:539) *Here Audubon has shown the Trumpeter Swan, aptly named for its percussive cry, foraging for food. Later Robert Havell added the bird's insect prey to the engraving of this image.*

The largest waterfowl in North America, Trumpeter Swans were prized and slaughtered in the nineteenth century for their elegant feathers, which served a variety of practical and ornamental purposes, from quill pens to powder puffs. Almost extinct at the beginning of this century, the Trumpeter Swan population has been restored by conservation measures in the Northwest, but it is now rarely seen along the Missouri, where Audubon observed it in 1843.

is stunned in ascent. As in Audubon's composition, the birds' outspread wings and splayed feet record their disarray.

In a way that Audubon does not, Homer includes details to identify all the protagonists involved, and to underline the character of the drama depicted. A small boat, which is set on the crest of the surf in the background, carries the marksman and his companion (sometimes considered to be Homer), who are stalking the prey. The artist provides a brilliant dab of orange amidst some gray smoke to make explicit the gunfire that has interrupted the flight of the pair of ducks, thereby not only identifying who is responsible for the mayhem but also highlighting the immediacy of the event. In *Right and Left*, Homer provides an agitated ocean setting as a visual counterpoint to the conflict of hunter and prey. Nature itself participates in the suggestion of aggression with its turbulent surf tossing up icy serrated knives of the white ocean spray toward the feet of the wounded birds. Although Homer presents the theme in a more explicit fashion, both artists use their images of the Goldeneye to suggest the elemental opposition of man and nature. Since both men were enthusiastic hunters, it is uncertain whether their paintings of conflict were intended to emphasize the heroism of the aggressor or the vulnerability of the prey. The symbolic interpretation is left to the beholder.

Audubon shows little awareness of vulnerability in his image of the *Trumpeter Swan* (p. 105), a bird that he knew well. It was different aspects of the bird that caught his fancy. He had frequently observed this giant swan, the largest in the world and a native of North America, in the wild, and he kept one as a pet for his children for two years during their stay in Henderson, Kentucky. His image emphasizes the muscularity, rather than the fragility or grace, of this waterfowl. Its thick, strong neck is bent back in a double S-curve against its massive breast. The opened bill and focused eye are directed toward an invisible aquatic insect, soon to be ingested, that would appear in the water when the drawing was transferred to copperplate. When resting in the sun, Audubon noticed that the Trumpeter Swan "draws one foot expanded curiously towards the back, and in that posture remains often for half an hour at a time," as he represents it here.[78] Two aspects of swan behavior are combined in one image; the tail end is depicted at rest and the front end in a position of active attack. A kind of composite life history of the bird is molded into a single form.

Because of its large size and splendid plumage, the Trumpeter Swan was a valuable trophy for hunters. Its eggs and young were gathered for food, while its feathers were sold to make decorative accessories, powder puffs, down for quilts, and quills for pens. Audubon acknowledged that, in depicting the feet and claws of small birds, he used the Trumpeter's quills because of their superior qualities. "They were so hard, and yet so elastic," he wrote enthusiastically, "that the best steel-pen of the present day might have blushed, if it could, to be compared with them."[79] Such commercial uses of its plumage were beginning to diminish the numbers of the Trumpeter Swan in Audubon's day, but the artist showed the concern of a hunter rather than a conservationist in his estimation of the bird. "Unless you have a good gun well loaded with large buck-shot," he noted, "you

Alexander Pope (1849–1924), *The Trumpeter Swan*

1911. Oil on canvas, 57¼ × 43¾″.
Signed lower left: Alexander Pope—11.
Meredith Long Gallery, Houston, Texas, 1972.
Private Collection, 1980.

Best known for his trompe l'oeil pictures (or door still lifes), Alexander Pope was also one of several artists depicting hanging game in the late nineteenth and early twentieth centuries. Unlike many other game artists, however, Pope was a committed conservationist, and The Trumpeter Swan *(1911), which hung for many years in the Massachusetts Society for the Prevention of Cruelty to Animals, has been interpreted as a denunciation of the near extinction of this species. The bird's outstretched wings and hanging neck recall a crucifixion scene, and they provide a sharp contrast to Audubon's picturesque portrayal of the swimming Trumpeter Swan (see p. 105).*

Common Goldeneye

Audubon's name: Golden-eye Duck. c. 1832–34.
Watercolor, graphite, and black and brown pastel
on paper, 21³⁄₁₆ × 29⅝".
Collection of The New-York Historical Society.

This unusual watercolor shows a pair of Common Goldeneyes interrupted in flight moments after the male, in front, has been wounded in the wing. Audubon was an avid hunter, and clearly did not shy from depicting the subject. "The flight of this species is powerful, extremely rapid, and wonderfully protracted," he wrote admiringly of these remarkable aviators. "It passes along with a speed equal to that of any Duck tribe, and I believe can easily traverse the space of ninety miles in an hour. The whistling of its wings may be distinctly heard when it is more than half a mile distant." (Ornithological Biography, *4:321*)

Audubon probably made this watercolor between 1832 and 1834 while on the Atlantic coast. He had painted the duck at least two other times in more straightforward profile portraits, typical of his early style. Through his frequent travels, he would have become familiar with the Common Goldeneye, which is present in abundance in the eastern United States—inland on forested lakes and rivers, moving south to salt bays and the ocean shores during the winter.

Winslow Homer (1836–1910).
Right and Left

1909. Oil on canvas, 28¼ × 48⅜″.
National Gallery of Art, Washington, D.C.

Winslow Homer's Right and Left *of
1909 recalls Audubon's depiction of the
Common Goldeneye, painted seventy-five
years earlier. Both paintings present the
ducks in a pair, seen from an elevated and
immediate vantage point, at the moment
they are being fired upon by a hunter below
in the distance (not seen in the Audubon
image). In each work, one duck is beginning to plunge downward as the other
rises in startled flight. While Homer was
probably influenced by Audubon's image
of the ducks, Audubon's painting shows
greater attention to precise details of the
duck's appearance, while Homer focused
on the drama of the moment.*

may shoot at them without much effect, for they are strong and tough birds."[80]

A trompe l'oeil image of the *Trumpeter Swan* (p. 107) by the American artist and active preservationist Alexander Pope, painted in 1911, suggests that artist's fear for the survival of the species by that date. Pope shows the dead bird suspended with its head facing the floor against a paneled door, carpeted with ivy and bisected diagonally by the shotgun that brought it down. With wings and tail outspread as if in flight, the artist emphasizes the still suspension of the graceful bird. It becomes an object for contemplation, a senseless *memento mori*, the reminder of a needless death.

Although Audubon did not focus on the issue of species preservation in every image that he made of birds whose numbers were diminishing, his entire enterprise sought to immortalize the abundance and beauty of the feathered inhabitants of the American wilderness. He knew that both the birds and their pristine environment were mutable. He shared an apprehension about the spread of civilization across the land with such contemporary Hudson River painters as Thomas Cole (1801–1848) and Frederic Church (1826–1900). In his "Essay on American Scenery," published in 1835, Cole considered the qualities of the American landscape and their relationship to scenes in the Old World. In his view, the most distinctive characteristic of nature in America was its "wildness." Untouched by the civilizing intrusion of man, nature in the New World retained the imprint of Creation. It was still freshly molded by the Creator's hand and through this direct spiritual connection remained "a fitting place to speak of God." Voicing his own apprehension at civilization's progressive encroachment on the wilderness, Cole wrote, "I cannot but express my sorrow that the beauty of such landscapes are quickly passing away—the ravages of the axe are daily increasing—the most noble scenes are made desolate, and oftentimes with a wantonness and barbarism scarcely credible in a civilized nation. The way-side is becoming shadeless, and another generation will behold spots, now rife with beauty, desecrated by what is called improvement."[81]

The landscape artists often pictured autumnal, Edenic views of uninhabited nature at twilight, suggesting through the season and the time of day that the end of such pristine settings was near. Frederic Church, a pupil of Thomas Cole, painted such an idyllic scene in 1860 and titled it *Twilight in the Wilderness* (p. 124). The fiery red clouds of the sunset sky dominate the composition, dwarfing the darkened calm of the uninhabited landscape below. A gentle river, its banks blanketed with late summer vegetation, meanders slowly into the distant hills on the western horizon. In the left foreground, perched atop the highest branch of a tree denuded of leaves, is a small bird. Its tiny form, silhouetted against the evening sky, stands as both a witness to and a symbol of the passing glory of the wilderness.

With these landscape painters, Audubon shared mixed feelings about the value of progress. Sometimes he applauded the courage of frontiersmen in confronting the dangers of the wild and paving routes for others to follow safely. At other times, he regretted the passage of the "grandeur and beauty of those almost uninhabited shores." Audubon declined final judgment on the spread of civilization across the American continent. "Whether these changes are for the better or for the worse," he demurred, "I shall not pretend to say."[82] However, he was unequivocal about the necessity of preserving the "original state" of the country for posterity, and *The Birds of America* was one part of his contribution toward that goal.

The Double Elephant Folio edition of *The Birds of America* had secured for Audubon an undisputed reputation in both Europe and America as a superior natural artist. William Swainson, the British scientist, praised the publication of large engravings for achieving "a perfection in the higher attributes of zoological painting, never before attempted."[83] On this side of the Atlantic, the diarist and one-time mayor of New York, Philip Hone (1780–1851) lavished similar praise on Audubon and his work, saying that *The Birds of America* was the greatest work on the subject ever produced. Alexander Wilson's *American Ornithology* deserved praise, admitted Hone, "beautiful, no doubt, but comparing with Audubon's as the Falls of Trenton to those of Niagara."[84] In fact, Hone found Audubon's publication so exceptional as to merit the status of a national treasure. He suggested that a copy be purchased by the federal government to form the nucleus of a national museum.

In spite of the fame and honor that the publication of the elephant folio edition of *The Birds of America* brought to Audubon, it did not make him rich nor, indeed, financially secure. The project was a long and expensive one. It took Audubon approximately twelve years to complete and, by his estimate, cost him about $115,000 to produce. With all the effort that he and his entire family devoted to gathering subscribers, about one hundred sixty complete sets were ultimately sold. Some additional incomplete bound sets and loose sets of prints were also sold, making an official accounting imprecise. His profit over the twelve-year period was somewhere in the range of $50,000 to $70,000.

To make the project more profitable and to distribute the publication to a wider audience, Audubon had planned for some time to publish a smaller, octavo edition of *The Birds of America*. With the help of a *camera lucida*—an apparatus that projected and reduced the bird images from one sheet to another, to facilitate tracing—and the lithographer John T. Bowen, Audubon was able to reproduce, on sheets approximately one-eighth the size of the large Elephant Folio sheets (about 10¾ by 7 inches), a smaller copy of the larger publication at a relatively low cost. He made some changes in the new "miniature edition." The arrangement of the octavo plates followed the scientific relationship of genera and species as they were understood by Audubon, rather than the unscientific sequence of the Elephant Folio. He also added some new plates and combined some of the original images. The hand-colored lithographs (about five hundred in all, gathered into one hundred fascicules of five plates each) were accompanied by text taken from his *Ornithological Biographies* describing the birds' habits, anatomy, digestive processes, and local habitats. He omitted the prose essays, or "delineations of American Scenery."

The success of this publication outstripped Audubon's grandest expectations. Having originally ordered three hundred copies of the prints, Audubon

Key west Pigeon.
COLUMBA MONTANA.
Male 1 Female 2

Key West Quail-Dove

Audubon's name: Key West Pigeon. 1832. Robert Havell, engraver.
Hand-colored etching and aquatint, 20¾ × 25⅞".
New York Public Library.

In the watercolor for this engraving, Audubon depicted a pair of Key West Quail-Doves (the male on the left) set against a background, drawn by his assistant George Lehman, of morning glories and flowers of the sweet potato vine. In the foreground is a cluster of leaves collaged onto the composition to enhance the design for engraving.

Audubon first saw the Key West Quail-Dove on May 6, 1832, during his visit to Key West, when his guide shot one of these birds for him. He recorded in his journal for that day that this "Pigeon which I had never seen" was "the most beautiful yet found in the United States. How I gazed on its resplendent plumage!—how I marked the expression of its rich-coloured, large and timid eye." (Ornithological Biography, 2:383) *He added, "The flight of this bird is low, swift, and protracted. I saw several afterwards when they were crossing from Cuba to Key West, the only place in which I found them."* (Ornithological Biography, 2:384) *Indeed, the Key West Quail-Dove is not indigenous to Florida but is actually a West Indian vagrant that sometimes makes its way to southern Florida.*

American Flamingo

Audubon's name: American Flamingo. 1838.
Watercolor, selective glazing, graphite, and gouache
on paper, 33³⁄₁₆ × 24¹⁄₈".
Collection of The New-York Historical Society.

*When Audubon first caught sight of a
flock of flamingoes in flight off the southeastern coast of Florida, his delight
matched his anticipation of the moment.
"Far away to seaward we spied a flock of
flamingoes advancing in 'Indian line'
with well spread wings, outstretched
necks, and long legs directed backwards,"
he noted. "Ah! Reader, could you but
know the emotions that then agitated my
breast! I thought I had now reached the
height of all my expectations, for my voyage to the Floridas was undertaken in a
great measure for the purpose of studying
these lovely birds in their own beautiful
islands." (*Ornithological Biography,
5:255*) Although Audubon was eager to
draw the flamingo following his first sighting in 1832, it was not until 1838 that
he was finally able to procure specimens
from Cuba and complete this painting.*

had to increase the printing to over one thousand copies within a few months to satisfy the demand of subscribers. The astonishing profits prompted Audubon to refer to the octavo edition, among the most successful subscriptions of the nineteenth century, as his "salvator."

The most tangible evidence of the smaller publication's financial rewards was Audubon's purchase, in 1841, of thirty to forty acres on the banks of the Hudson River in an area of upper Manhattan now known as Audubon Terrace. He built a house on the property, which he called "Minnie's Land" in honor of his wife, Lucy, who was known as Minnie to her children (p. 125). Ultimately, a barn, a painting studio, a stable, dairy, and poultry yards, enclosures for foxes, deer, elk, and wolves, and houses for his sons were erected on this pastoral, wooded, riverside retreat from the city. Audubon said that he could never understand why "men can consent to swelter and fret their lives away amid those hot bricks and pestilent vapors, when the woods and fields are all so near?"[85] The royal octavo edition of *The Birds of America* gave him the financial security to escape the "crazy city" and provide his family with a homestead, a place where many of them would later remember happy times together.

Audubon began work on a new publication while he was producing the "miniature" edition of *The Birds of America*. He enlisted the help of John Bachman to undertake a comprehensive work devoted to the mammals of North America. Bachman agreed to help, but warned that the task would prove far more difficult than Audubon imagined; because little had been written on the subject, long study journeys were required, and many specimens had to be obtained. "I think I have studied the subject more than you have," wrote Bachman to Audubon. "You will be bothered with the Wolves and Foxes, to begin with. . . . The Western Deer are no joke, and the ever varying Squirrels seem sent by Satan himself to puzzle the Naturalists."[86]

Audubon embarked on the project with confidence, no doubt because he had the successful *The Birds of America* publication to his credit. He was now a mature artist with an established methodology and a style of work that met his own exacting standards, as well as those of his audience. Moreover, he was attempting a subject that was not entirely new to him. He had been depicting animals, at least occasionally, all of his life. At an early age, he had made a profile portrait of a *Marmot* (p. 12, top). A number of his hunting pictures, painted in oil for English collectors in the 1820s, included mammals. The *Entrapped Otter* (p. 72), a dramatic and poignant subject, that Audubon copied several times, provided a posture that the artist adapted to some of his later mammal drawings. A comparison of the otter with the watercolors of the *Bobcat* (p. 128) and the *Wolverine* (p. 129) shows that the animals are presented in similar side views with their heads turned forward and teeth bared. Mammals had occasionally appeared as accessories in the bird portraits, especially as objects of prey (p. 130). The figure of an Eastern Grey Squirrel, drawn in 1821, was incorporated as a victim of harassment in the engraved plate of the *Barred Owl* (p. 116), and ultimately became an independent subject in the *Viviparous Quadrupeds of North America* (p. 36).

By January 1840, even before Bachman agreed to take on the authorship of

Woodchuck

1841. Watercolor and pencil on paper, 23 × 33¹¹⁄₁₆".
Pierpont Morgan Library, New York.

Audubon pictures a female woodchuck and her young—a species of marmot he admired for its "power of escaping the rigours and cold blasts of that season, and resting securely, in a sleep of insensibility, free from all cravings of hunger and danger of perishing of cold, till the warm sun of spring once more calls them into life and activity." (Quadrupeds, 1:21) The young woodchuck at the left bears close resemblance to one of Audubon's earliest extant drawings of the same species, done in 1805.

The hibernating woodchuck, which can be found throughout Canada as well as the northeastern and midwestern United States, lives in a den or burrow and feeds on various grasses and plants. Active during the day or night, woodchucks often climb trees to rest in the sunshine and sometimes raid gardens or fields for food.

Great Gray Owl

Audubon's name: Great Cinereous Owl. Probably c. 1834–36. Robert Havell, engraver.
Hand-colored etching and aquatint, 38 × 25¼".
New York Public Library.

"*This fine owl, which is the largest of the North American species, is nowhere common with us, although it ranges from the north-eastern coast of the United States to the sources of the Columbia River.*" The rarity of the Great Gray Owl compelled Audubon to make his drawing from a specimen in the collection of the Zoological Society of London, since he was unable to procure a bird in the wild. (Ornithological Biography, 4:364)

The Great Gray Owl is indeed the largest North American owl, due to the bulk of its feathers. It preys on small birds and mammals and often hunts in the daytime. The owl lives primarily in the forests and bordering meadows of Canada, and can be quite tame.

Roseate Tern

Audubon's name: Roseate Tern. 1832. Robert Havell, engraver.
Hand-colored etching and aquatint, 19½ × 12¼″.
New York Public Library.

"The Roseate Tern is at all times a noisy, restless bird," Audubon observed. "On approaching its breeding place, it incessantly emits its sharp shrill cries, resembling the syllable crak. Its flight is unsteady and flickering," which caused Audubon to call them Hummingbirds of the Sea. "They would dash at us and be off again with astonishing quickness, making great use of their tail on such occasions. While in search of prey, they carry the bill in the manner of the Common Tern, that is perpendicularly downward, plunge like a shot, with wings nearly closed, so as to immerse part of the body, and immediately reascend. They were seen dipping in this manner eight or ten times in succession, and each time generally secured a small fish." (Ornithological Biography, 3:297–298)

The adult tern shown in this plate, with its spring season pink breast, was cut out from a separate drawing and added to the blue background.

the *Quadruped* text, Audubon was spending all his time painting animals and procuring specimens. He worked usually about fourteen hours a day in a room that was situated to the left of the broad entry hall at Minnie's Land in the traditional position of the parlor. "It was not, however, a parlor, or any ordinary reception-room," recorded one visitor to Audubon's work room. "In one corner stood a painter's easel, with a half-finished sketch of a beaver on paper; in the other lay the skin of an American Panther. The antlers of elks hung upon the walls, stuffed birds of every description of gay plumage ornamented the mantle-piece; and exquisite drawings of field-mice, orioles, and woodpeckers were scattered promiscuously in other parts of the room."[87]

While Audubon could boast, almost with complete truth, that every image in *The Birds of America* was drawn from life by his own hand, he did not make a similar claim for the *Quadrupeds*. He depended to a great extent upon skins and mounted animals sent to him by a variety of correspondents and institutions. To acquire a specimen for his watercolor painting of the *Snowshoe Hare* (p. 132), Audubon had to instruct Increase S. Smith of Hingham, Massachusetts, in the method of preserving the mammal from putrefaction during shipment. "The animals ought to be put in a Keg of Common Yankee Rum," wrote Audubon, "and as soon as possible after death, cutting a slit in the abdomen of not exceeding *Two Inches* in length, and pouring Rum in the aperture until well filled. The Entrails must remain untouched."[88]

During 1840–41, while Audubon was hard at work traveling, selling subscriptions, and producing drawings for the *Quadrupeds,* a series of tragedies befell his family. In September 1840, Maria Bachman, the wife of his younger son John Woodhouse, died after less than three years of marriage. That same autumn, Eliza Bachman married his older son Victor and the following spring she too died. Since Audubon had lost his two daughters when they were very small, these young women held a special place in his affections, and he was profoundly saddened by their passing. An inscription on his watercolor drawing of the *Gray Rabbit* records the depth of his loss (p. 133). "I drew this Hare during one of the days of deepest sorrow I have felt in my life and my only solace was derived from my labour—This morning our beloved daughter Eliza died at 2 o'clock—She is now in Heaven, and may our God forever bless her soul!" Clearly, the intense pace of his work during these years served, in part, as a distraction from the illnesses and deaths occurring in his family.

In making the drawings for the *Quadrupeds,* as well as in securing specimens, Audubon relied upon the assistance of his sons to a greater extent than he had with *The Birds of America. Northern Hare* by John James Audubon (p. 134) and its background (p. 135, top), by his older son Victor Gifford, offer a graphic illustration of the collaboration of Audubon and his sons on the *Quadruped* publication. The two images are combined in the lithograph with the delineation of the sky omitted; the total effect is more sharply focused, due the shift from watercolor and oil to lithography (p. 135, bottom). The older artist represented hares as muscular animals activated by their crouched and leaping postures. Their eyes, paws, and whiskers are delineated in fine detail. Audubon traced the individual bristles of the hares' soft coats with single strokes of a pen over the water-color soft fur. The tactile finish of the animals' coats was a consistent concern of the artist in all of his images of animals. He implored the printer of the *Quadrupeds* "not to forget *to hair the backs* of each figure very finely and long," in a plate depicting a group of black rats feasting on eggs (p. 136).[89]

In keeping with his training as a landscape artist, Audubon's son Victor treated the background for the hares in a loose, brushy style to offset the sharply focused rendering of the animals. No specific habitat or locale is indicated, but an inscription within the outline of the larger hare instructs the printer that "these animals *must* be given as here/without the *least* reduction in size." In addition to providing many of the backgrounds or plant accessories to his father's paintings of mammals, Victor acted as business manager for the project. He supervised the transference of the original paintings to stone and made sure that the prints were exact in their design and color.

However, it was Audubon's younger son "Johnny," trained as a portraitist, who would eventually take over the task of the *Quadrupeds* as his father's health declined, traveling to Texas, Canada, and Britain to seek animal specimens for inclusion in the work. Eventually, in 1846, he would take on the sole responsibility for producing almost half the plates when his father's deteriorating health prevented him from carrying his final work to completion.

The series of images of squirrels (pp. 137, 138, and 139) indicate that the senior Audubon often achieved, in the animal paintings by his own hand, the same lively expression in the subjects and variety of composition as he had with the birds. Within the limited format of a couple of tree branches and a few squirrels, the artist constantly modifies the poses, facial expressions, and interactions of his subjects. He delights our eye with the curve of a tail, the reach of a paw, or the twist of a head. What an unforgettable image Audubon makes in the *Cat Squirrel* (p. 139) with the specimen at the top of the composition. The animal grips the branch in a steel-like embrace with its hind feet and wraps its body downward around the support. Audubon conveys his wonder at the squirrel's acrobatic climbing technique, which he had probably observed frequently first-hand. In 1843, a writer for the Boston *Atlas* praised the vitality of Audubon's animal drawings, especially his images of squirrels which "are so thoroughly life itself, that few people would venture to put their fingers near the mouth of one of the squirrels, for fear of an actual bite."[90]

Audubon admired the variety of coloring in the Cat Squirrel, and the distinct orange, gray, and black tints displayed in this drawing record the wide range of color possibility within a single species, at least as it was understood by the artist. However, Audubon was not sure about the significance of color in identifying species. "I am greatly at a loss to say positively whether the different colours form specific distinctions," he wrote uncertainly. "I should like therefore to find their nests & their young to assure myself before actually writing much or pertinently on the subject."[91] With the help of John Bachman, the *Viviparous Quadrupeds of North America* included twenty-four species of tree squirrels, although many of the common and Latin names that they were assigned are no longer in use. Bachman bemoaned the fact that they were unable to give a complete representation of American mammals; whales, seals, and bats were omitted. However, the completeness of some other groups such as carnivores, insectivores, rodents, and hoofed animals made the *Quadrupeds* the unrivaled authority of its time.

When he showed his plates to prospective subscribers to the *Quadrupeds* publication, Audubon was astonished at the ignorance many people displayed about the identity of North American mammals. Since they were entrusted with the responsibility of approving the subscription expenditure for the Library of Congress, members of the United States Congress reviewed some sample *Quadruped* plates. They demonstrated a shocking lack of familiarity with even the most common animal species. "The Great Folks call the Rats Squirrels, the squirrels flying ones, and the Marmots, poor things, are regularly called Beavers or Musk Rats," wrote Audubon with astonishment. Since one senator did not recognize the artist until his name was announced, Audubon speculated, jokingly, that "I might have passed for a Beaver or a Musk Rat in his eye for aught I know."[92]

Who could fail to recognize the woodchuck, a species of marmot, after looking at Audubon's preparatory watercolor and pencil sketch showing the animal in a variety of postures to expose its characteristic parts? (p. 115) Having kept a woodchuck in a cage for several weeks to observe its habits, Audubon was anxious to infuse his image with this intimate acquaintance. Subtle color modulations render the variety of tone that identifies different parts of the mammals' bodies including brown, red, ochre, grey, tan, and russet. Fine pencil and ink lines scratched on the surface reproduce the texture of fur, hair by hair. As his notes on the drawing reveal, certain body parts such as the teeth claimed Audubon's particular attention. By including a profile and a frontal view of the animal, the artist could show both "incisors seen in front/incisors seen sideways." The feet and their positions were similarly noted on the drawing. More commentary about the habits of the woodchuck are inscribed on the recto of the sheet. The artist records the woodchuck's shrill whistle in response to danger that is followed by "a sort of maniacal laugh . . . as if in a severe fit of ague." At rest, which was infrequent, the woodchucks adopted the posture of squirrels by sitting erect on their rumps and letting their forelegs and feet hang loosely, as Audubon discovered and described in this drawing. In this position, they appear approachable and affectionate, but according to Audubon they are aggressive and even savage. The live woodchucks in his care tried to gnaw their way out of the strong wire cage with their teeth, "at the cost of the latter, which broke almost to the roots." Audubon left the background blank for the lithographer to complete and the print shows the animals situated on the ground with grasses and a few small plants lending a sense of scale to the subjects.

By 1842, Audubon decided that the need for specimens and information about mammal species in the western portions of the country required an exploratory trip. He hoped to make a significant contribution to science by identifying from first-hand experience hitherto unknown species of quadrupeds native to the western region. Writing to his colleague and friend Charles Bonaparte in February 1843, Audubon explained that "to render this new Work the more compleate, I will leave the comforts of my home and beloved family on the 10th of next month bound to the Rocky Mountains. I cannot tell how long I may be absent, but hope to return with knowledge new and abundance of Drawings made on the spot and not from stuffed-museums moth eaten remains."[93]

On a visit to Washington, D.C., he failed to get federal sponsorship for the trip. At Fuller's Hotel, where he was staying, however, he re-encountered an acquaintance from New York, Colonel Pierre Chouteau, owner of the American Fur Company. The fur company owned a trading post on the Missouri River and secured pelts through trade with the Indians in that region. With Chouteau's support and encouragement, Audubon determined to embark the following April on a fur company steamer setting out from St. Louis and traveling up the Missouri. He enlisted companions and helpers to accompany him on the trip. The ornithologist Edward Harris (1799–1863), a long-time friend, agreed to go, using the opportunity to prepare a report on the geology of the Upper Missouri for the Philadelphia Academy of Sciences. A year earlier, Audubon had met Isaac Sprague (1811–1895), an artist whose work he admired. He persuaded Sprague to come along and "assist me when wanted, [and] especially draw plants and Views for backgrounds for our present work."[94]

The party boarded the steamer *Omega* on April 25, 1843, for what would prove to be Audubon's last trip. "My head is actually swimming with excitement," the artist wrote, as he embarked upon his upstream journey. En route, he delighted in recording in his notebook the changing topography and the attendant diversity of animal and plant life on the shore. When the boat pulled ashore, the travelers disembarked to hunt, both for food and for sport. The region's plentiful game offered them ample opportunities. "I never saw so many rabbits and partridges," Audubon reported in a letter to a friend. "To give you an idea, upwards of 50 rabbits and some squirrels were shot in less than three hours. The ground hogs were equally numerous but kept to their holes. . . . Almost every green spot along the hill-sides has its gangs of buffaloes . . . the antelopes are beautiful small animals and run like the wind, but not so fast as a rifle-ball."

Even as he exulted at the thrill of hunting, however, Audubon protested wanton killing for sport. He observed prairies littered with the carcasses of buffalo, brought down for nothing more than the harvest of their tongues. His journals reflect that, on some occasions, he indulged without remorse in hunting for sport, while on others he worried about the extinction of species and the passing of the wilderness. However, the conflicts he experienced as a naturalist/hunter were leisure-time musings. These private reflections, scribbled into his notebook at the end of the day did not compel resolution. Audubon's principal and public focus during his western trip, and all his other exploratory journeys, was to contribute new information to science, for which he would be accountable. "I have some hopes of making a decent trip of it for the sake of science," he remarked, "but it will be a dear one to my poor purse."[95]

After fifty days of travel, the party arrived on June 13 at Fort Union, a trading outpost just above the mouth of the Yellowstone River. Two busy months at

John James Audubon's prints
shipping box

Courtesy, Department of Library Services,
American Museum of Natural History, New York.

合衆國有名の禽學者奥度棒ある時旅行して家を多年思慮を殫して模寫せる粉本を箱に入親戚に托し一置き數月にして家に帰り箱を開き見るに鼠其内に巣くひ画圖は悉く齧まれて碎片となれり奥度棒は是を見て大に心を傷ましり数日の間恍惚として失態せる者の如し既みるに又舊の如くに鋭と手にし一記簿鉛筆を携へ林に入て禽鳥を捕へ其形狀を模寫せしが三年に画又箱に満ち模寫も前時より更に好きを覚えしとて

A Japanese Portrait of John James Audubon, finding Two Hundred of his Bird Drawings Destroyed by Rats.

Published, 1878. Woodcut, 14¼ × 9⁷⁄₁₆″.
Collection of The New-York Historical Society.

This woodcut from The Western Countries Book of Successful Careers, *published in 1878 in Japan, dramatically depicts a confrontation between Audubon and a family of Norway Rats. The mishap involved a box of two hundred bird paintings stored at the farm of a friend, Dr. Adam Rankin, in Henderson, Kentucky, during one of Audubon's trips. While in storage, the bird paintings were destroyed by Norway Rats which used them as material for a nest inside the box.*

Audubon's wife, Lucy, and his young son Victor had stayed with the Rankins, with Lucy acting as tutor to the Rankin children, in December 1810 to April 1811 while Audubon was away. The Audubons visited Lucy's family at Fatland Ford, the Bakewell family plantation in Pennsylvania, from December 1811 to early summer of 1812, with Audubon making trips to Philadelphia for business. It was probably on the return from Pennsylvania to Kentucky that Audubon discovered the ruined drawings, kept in a chest during his absence.

Frederic Church. *Twilight in the Wilderness*

1860. Oil on canvas, 40 × 64″.
The Cleveland Museum of Art.

William Rickarby Miller
(1850–1923). *Minnie's Land, the
Audubon Residence on West 155th
Street in Carmansville on the
Hudson*

1865. Lithograph from the newspaper *Valentine's
Manual.*
Museum of the City of New York.

*This lithograph after a watercolor by
William Rickarby Miller shows the
Audubon house by the side of the Hudson
River. Known today as Audubon Terrace,
the area is now well within the borders of
New York City. During Audubon's time,
however, the estate represented a rural
escape from the noise and commotion of
the city still to the south of it.*

*The Audubon family moved to the resi-
dence on the Hudson in 1842, after two
years in New York City. They called it
"Minnie's Land" after Audubon's wife,
Lucy, and it was, in fact, deeded to her at
the time of the purchase. ("Minnie," a
Scottish term of endearment for "Mother,"
was the name by which Lucy was known
to her sons.) Audubon's granddaughter
Maria later reminisced about the pleasure
the artist had derived from fishing in the
river and from "the dense woods all
around [that] resounded to the songs of
the birds he so loved." (Journals,
1:71–72) Although Audubon continued
to travel—most notably, on the Missouri*

*in 1843—after settling at Minnie's
Land, he spent the last years of his life
there with his sons, who helped him complete his work on the* Quadrupeds of
North America.

*The house was demolished in 1932 to
make way for construction of the Riverside
Drive Viaduct. Along the viaduct, the site
of Audubon's house is now occupied by
apartment buildings; also on his former
property are the classically styled buildings
housing the Hispanic Society of America,
the American Academy of Arts and Letters, and the American Numismatic Society, at 156th Street.*

Swift Fox

Audubon's name: Kit Fox or Swift Fox. 1844.
Watercolor on paper, 29 × 24⅞".
Courtesy, Department of Library Services,
American Museum of Natural History, New York.

While Audubon believed the Swift Fox and Kit Fox to be two names for the same animal, they are actually two similar species. The Swift Fox is found in the Great Plains states, while the Kit Fox lives in the deserts west of the Rockies. Audubon came across the Swift Fox during his Missouri River expedition in 1843. Despite its name, Audubon wrote that "there is nothing in the conformation of this species, anatomically viewed, indicating extraordinary speed. On the contrary, when we compare it with the Red fox or even the Gray, we find its body and legs shorter in proportion than in those species, and its large head and bushy tail give it rather a more heavy appearance than either of the foxes just named." (Quadrupeds, 2:16)

Canada Lynx

Watercolor on paper, 42½ × 36″.
Courtesy, Department of Library Services, American
Museum of Natural History, New York.

*Audubon came across the Canada Lynx, a
wild bob-tailed cat, during his trip to
Labrador in 1833 and remarked upon its
diminishing numbers due to trapping.
"The skin of this animal is generally used
for muffs, collars, &c., and is ranked
among the most beautiful materials for these
purposes. . . . Savage and voracious as he
may be when pursuing the smaller animals,
[the lynx] is equally cowardly when opposed
to his great enemy—man; and as his skin is
valuable, let us excuse him for desiring to
keep it whole."* (Quadrupeds, *1:139,
141*)

*The lynx is well equipped for its northern
habitat with a heavy coat and large feet
which act as snowshoes.* "It is very strong
and possessing remarkably large and powerful fore-legs and claws," *wrote Audubon,*
"is able to climb trees of any size, and can
leap from a considerable height to the
ground without feeling the jar."
(Quadrupeds, *1:140*)

Bobcat

Audubon's name: Common American Wild Cat or
Bay Lynx. 1842.
Watercolor on paper, 24¾ × 35⅞″.
Courtesy, Department of Library Services,
American Museum of Natural History, New York.

*"The Wild Cat pursues his prey with both
activity and cunning,"* Audubon wrote of
the bobcat, *"sometimes bounding suddenly
upon the object of his rapacity, sometimes
with stealthy pace, approaching it in the
darkness of night, seizing it with his
strong retractile claws and sharp teeth,
and bearing it off to his retreat in the forest."* (Quadrupeds, *1:6*) Similar to a
lynx but usually smaller, the bobcat hunts
small mammals and can be found from
southern Canada to central Mexico.
Shown here with a snarling expression,
the bobcat proved to be, in Audubon's
experience, a vicious and untameable animal. *"We once made an attempt at domes-
ticating one of the young of this species,
which we obtained when only two weeks
old. It was a most spiteful, growling,
snappish little wretch, and showed no dis-
position to improve its habits and manners under our kind tuition."*
(Quadrupeds, *1:14*)

Wolverine

Audubon's name: Wolverene or Glutton. Victor G.
Audubon (background). 1841.
Watercolor and oil on paper, 35¼ × 25".
Courtesy, Department of Library Services,
American Museum of Natural History, New York..

The first time Audubon ever saw a Wolverine, after following what he thought were bear tracks, he believed he had discovered a new species of quadruped. It was not until six months later that he discovered his error and confirmed that his "highly prized specimen" was the wolverine, "of which [he] had read such marvellous tales in the school-books." (Quadrupeds, 1:208)

After observing the animal, Audubon set out to discredit many of those "marvellous tales." "The wolverene, or glutton as he is generally called, is one of the animals whose history comes down to us blended with the superstitions of the old writers. . . . The wolverene, confined almost exclusively to Polar regions, where men have enjoyed few advantages of education and hence have imbibed without much reflection the errors, extravagances and inventions of hunters and trappers, has been represented as an animal possessing extraordinary strength, agility, and cunning, and as being proverbially one of the greatest gormandizers among the 'brutes.'" (Quadrupeds, 1:205) Audubon asserted, instead, that the wolverine was a more gentle creature that fed mainly on the carcasses of small animals killed by accident. The wolverine is now known to be a ferocious hunter who feeds on deer as well as smaller prey and will kill a moose or elk trapped in deep snow.

Black Vulture

Audubon's name: Black Vulture. Bird on left and
deer's head painted c. 1829; second bird added
later.
Watercolor, pastel, graphite, and collage on paper,
23⅜ × 36⅛".
Collection of The New-York Historical Society.

*Audubon remarked upon the presence of
Black Vultures in several cities in the
South, but he was careful to distinguish
among the habits of the birds as they
adapted to different areas. "I found this
species abundant in Texas, where it bred,
as usual, on the ground, but in situations
such as I had not before seen; for the nests
which I examined were under very small
bushes in marshes adjoining salt-water
lagoons, or amidst cactuses, and along
with several species of heron, the young of
these latter forming a considerable portion
of the food of the young Vultures."*
(Ornithological Biography, 5:346)

*One of Audubon's earlier observations
about the vultures, presented in a scientific paper in 1826, aroused some contro-
versy. He asserted that the birds rely on
sight rather than smell to locate the car-
rion on which they feed. His theory that
vultures have an undeveloped sense of
smell met resistance at the time but was
later confirmed through experiments.*

Common American Skunk

1842. Watercolor and pencil on paper, 33 × 24½″.
Pierpont Morgan Library, New York.

"There is no quadruped on the continent of North America," Audubon wrote, *"the approach of which is more generally detested than that of the skunk."* (Quadrupeds, *1:320*) More amused than annoyed, Audubon added that, *"not infrequently, even the bravest of our boasting race is by this little animal compelled suddenly to break off his train of thought,* hold his nose, *and run, as if a lion were at his heels!"* (Quadrupeds, *1:321*)

Audubon noted that the Skunk, despite its clean habits (it never allows the foul-smelling liquid to besmirch its own fur) is unpopular with farmers. An omnivore, it is particularly fond of eggs, and will consume fruit and corn. The striped skunk is found in cities as well woods, prairies, and suburbs, and is chiefly nocturnal.

Snowshoe Hare

Audubon's name: American Hare or Northern
Hare. 1842.
Watercolor on paper, pasted on cloth, 19 × 26″.
Courtesy, Department of Library Services,
American Museum of Natural History.

*Known to Audubon as the Northern Hare
or American Hare, and today more commonly called the Snowshoe Hare and
Varying Hare, this rabbit is found in the
woodlands and swamps of North America, from Canada and Alaska to the Rockies, Great Lakes, and Appalachians. It is
known as the Snowshoe Hare because of
its unusually wide feet. "In deep snows,"
wrote Audubon, "the animal is so light,
and is so well supported by its broad furry
feet, that it passes over the surface making
only a faint impression." (*Quadrupeds,
*1:96) The term "Varying Hare" derives
from the hare's gradual seasonal change
of coat, from brown in the summer to
white, with black-tipped ears, in the winter. Shown here in its winter pelage,
Audubon also depicted the hare in its summer colors.*

Gray Rabbit

1841. Watercolor and pencil on paper,
23⅞ × 34⁵⁄₁₆″.
Pierpont Morgan Library, New York.

The Gray rabbit was, according to Audubon, "the most common hare in the Atlantic States of America." A rabbit that "abounds in our woods and forests, even in their densest coverts," it remains a notorious pest to farmers and gardeners. In addition to ravaging the farmer's crops, it "not unfrequently divests the young trees in the nursery of their bark; it often makes inroads upon the kitchen-garden, feasting on the young green peas, lettuces, cabbages, &c., and doing a great deal of mischief; and when it has once had an opportunity of tasting these dainties, it becomes difficult to prevent its making a nightly visit to them." (Quadrupeds, 1:174–175)

Although this species of rabbit is among the most prolific, it is at the mercy of many enemies, including weasels, lynxes, foxes, hawks, owls, snakes, and dogs, as well as humans.

Northern Hare

Audubon's name: Snowshoe Hare; known also as
American Hare. 1841–1842.
Watercolor on paper 26 × 19".
Courtesy, Department of Library Services,
American Museum of Natural History, New York.

Victor Gifford Audubon. *Snowshoe Hare (Background
for American Hare in Summer).* 1841–42.
Watercolor on paper, 20½ × 34¾".
Courtesy, Department of Library Services,
American Museum of Natural History, New York.

John James Audubon and Victor Gifford Audubon.
Northern Hare. Printed and colored by J. T. Bowen,
Philadelphia, 1843. Hand-colored lithograph,
20½ × 34¾". Courtesy, Department of Library
Services, American Museum of Natural History,
New York.

*These two images of the Northern Hare in
its summer coat indicate the collaborative
process by which some of the lithographs
for the* Viviparous Quadrupeds of
North America *were made. Audubon's
son Victor Gifford Audubon (1809–
1860) painted the background for the
hares, leaving blank space, with inscribed
directions, within their outlines. Victor
Audubon frequently helped his father with
his various projects, from monitoring
Joseph Bartholomew Kidd's progress on
making oil copies of Audubon's watercolors in 1833, to supervising the quality
and schedule of Robert Havell's printing
of the plates for* The Birds of America,
*to drawing backgrounds for some of the
images in the publication on mammals
and traveling in an effort to raise subscriptions for it.*

*Audubon painted the hares, whose neg-
ative shapes appear in Victor's work,
against a blank background. The lithographer joined the two images in the print
to create a finished compostion.*

 PLATE XL.

Black Rat

Victor G. Audubon (background). 1842.
Watercolor and oil on paper, 21⅝ × 27½″.
Collection of The New-York Historical Society.

Audubon's scientific interest in mammals did not prevent him from addressing the public perception of some of his subjects. "The character of this species is so notoriously bad," he wrote of the Black Rat, "that were we to write a volume in its defence we would fail to remove those prejudices which are everywhere entertained against this thieving cosmopolite." He added, however, that, "this species is by no means so great a pest, or so destructive, as the Brown or Norway rat, which has in many parts of the country either driven off or exterminated it. The Black Rat, in con-

sequence, has become quite rare." (Quadrupeds, 1:190, 191)

Audubon has depicted the rats feasting on eggs in a hen-house. Although Audubon claimed to have seen barns and poultry houses that were infested with rats who did not disturb the eggs, he noted that this situation rarely lasted for long: "when . . . the rats once had a taste of the delicacies, they became as destructive as usual, and nothing could save the eggs or young fowls but making the buildings rat-proof, or killing the plunderers." (Quadrupeds, 1:191)

In this plate, Audubon has included three figures of a lighter-colored variety of the Black rat.

Red Squirrel/Downy Squirrel

Audubon's name: Downy Squirrel. 1841.
Watercolor on paper, pasted on linen, 21½ × 14⁹⁄₁₆".
Courtesy, Department of Library Services,
American Museum of Natural History, New York.

*Audubon believed his "Downy squirrel" to be a new species closely related to the Red Squirrel, and a "closely connecting link" between ground squirrels and tree squirrels. (*Quadrupeds, *1:200) In fact, the "Downy squirrel" is now considered to be a subspecies of the Red squirrel or Chickaree. He never observed a live "Downy squirrel," having received a specimen thirdhand from a trading post in British Columbia.*

Migratory Squirrel

1841. Watercolor and pencil on paper, 34¼ × 23⅞".
Pierpont Morgan Library, New York.

Audubon has depicted an old male squirrel actively moving along a low branch beneath a younger female. Known to Audubon as the Migratory Squirrel, because of its wide-ranging travels, or Sciurus leucotis, *this creature may now be recognized as part of the species* Sciurus carolinensus, *or the Common Gray Squirrel. Audubon regarded the animal as the "most active and sprightly species of squirrel" on the East Coast: "It sallies forth with the sun, and is industriously engaged in search of food for four or five hours in the morning. . . . In the middle of the day it retires for a few hours to its nest, resuming its active labours and amusements in the afternoon, and continuing them without intermission till long after the setting of the sun." (Quadrupeds, 1:267)*

Cat Squirrel

1841. Watercolor and pencil on paper, 36¾ × 24¼".
Pierpont Morgan Library, New York.

"Perhaps none of our squirrels are subject to greater varieties of colour than the present," Audubon remarked about the Cat squirrel. *"We have represented in the plate three of these Squirrels, all of different colours, but the varieties of tint to be observed in different specimens of the Cat squirrel, are so great, that among fifty or more perhaps, we never could find two exactly alike; for which reason we selected for our drawing an orange-coloured one, a gray one, and one nearly black."* (Quadrupeds, *1:146–147*) Audubon also observed that this squirrel was the least active of known species of squirrel. He believed that the sexes mated for life and *"the same pair, if undisturbed, may be found in a particular vicinity for a number of years in succession."* (Quadrupeds, *1:148*)

Raccoon

1841. Watercolor and pencil on paper, pasted on linen, 22¼ × 24¼".
Courtesy, Department of Library Services,
American Museum of Natural History, New York.

"The Raccoon which is a cunning and crafty animal, is found in all our woods," Audubon remarked, *"so that its name is familiar to every child in the Union."* (Ornithological Biography, *3:235*) *This mainly nocturnal animal, present in southern Canada and throughout most of the United States, does not hibernate but will hole up in a tree during extremely cold weather. It is well known for its dexterity. As Audubon noted of a raccoon kept as a pet: "It will adroitly pick its keeper's pockets of anything it likes to eat, and is always on the watch for dainties."* (Quadrupeds, *2:76*)

Porcupine

1842, Watercolor and pencil on paper, pasted on canvas, 25 × 34¼".
Courtesy, Department of Library Services, American Museum of Natural History, New York.

"Clothed in an impervious coat of mail bristling with bayonets," Audubon remarked that the porcupine *"can bid defiance to the whole ferine race, the grizzly bear not excepted."* (Quadrupeds, *1:280)* Despite its daunting armor, Audubon noted of a porcupine in his care for six months: *"It had become very gentle, and evinced no spiteful propensities; when we called to it, holding in our hand a tempting sweet-potatoe (sic) or apple, it would turn its head slowly towards us, and give us a mild and wistful look, and then with stately steps advance and take the fruit from our hand. . . . If it found the door of our study open, it would march in, and gently approach us, rubbing its sides against our legs, and looking up at us as if supplicating for additional delicacies."* (Quadrupeds, *1:280–281)*

Audubon encountered porcupines during his expedition to Labrador in 1833 and his trip to the upper Missouri River in 1843. A tree-climber active chiefly at night, the porcupine feeds on tree bark, buds, and twigs. It can be found in the woods of Canada, Alaska, and the northeastern and western United States.

the fort record hunting exploits, observations of Indians and trappers, and records of work accomplished. Audubon identified at least fourteen new species of birds, which could be incorporated in later editions of *The Birds of America*. He brought home the heads of antelopes, Big Horns, wolves, and buffaloes, as well as sketches of scenery and flowers, but the booty of new quadruped species was disappointing. "The variety of Quadrupeds is small in the Country we visited," he wrote dejectedly, "and I fear that I have not more than 3 or 4 New ones."[96] The river trip home was much more difficult and took far longer than expected because of violent adverse winds. The travelers were annoyed at night by wolves howling and buffaloes bellowing, but they were never attacked or even disturbed by Indians. On one occasion when they were obliged to tie up at the shore to avoid adverse weather, they killed a Grizzly Bear, which was an exciting event for Audubon. It gave him the direct experience that allowed him to report with conviction that he returned to Minnie's Land on November 5, 1843, "as fat as a Grisly Bear in good season."[97]

On his return home, his rough, unruly appearance so impressed his son John that he insisted his father allow him to capture his likeness in a portrait. (opposite). While Audubon clearly agreed to have himself rendered as an unshaven woodsman, he donned an elegant fur-trimmed coat to prevent the Grizzly Bear comparison from going too far.

Pain in Audubon's eyes and a deterioration of sight were the first symptoms of serious illness. He became unable to read or write and, more importantly, to paint. By 1848 when Bachman visited his old friend, he was shocked to find that although "the outlines of his countenance & his general robust form are there, the mind is all in ruins." Describing a deterioration of mental faculties that suggests Alzheimer's disease, Bachman observed sadly that the senior Audubon resembled "a crabbed restless uncontrollable child—worrying & bothering every one. He thinks of nothing but eating—scarcely sits down two minutes at a time, hides hens' eggs—rings the bell every five minutes calling the people to dinner . . . but I turn away from the subject with a feeling of sadness."[98] When Audubon died at Minnie's Land on January 27, 1851, aged 65, he still appeared strong, but his mind had lost touch with reality for over three years. His family buried him in the churchyard of Trinity Chapel at 155th Street and Broadway, where a tall runic cross erected some years later still stands to mark his grave. Ironically, it carries a mistaken birth date.

As his 1843 portrait confirms, Audubon was a man of multiple personae. He often commented that he was equally comfortable sleeping on the dirt ground with just a blanket to cover him as under the downy quilt of an elaborate European bed. He delighted in playing the violin and dancing in the parlor as much as trading tall tales and bawdy stories with the rough men he met in the wilderness. Sometimes he was a victim of the mercurial ebb and flow of his own self-confidence. In spite of his respectable European background, he could feel insecure and inferior, and withdraw into himself in the sophisticated and wealthy social circles that he frequented abroad in order to sell his subscriptions. Alternately, with the suave control of a professional actor, he could play the part of a

John Woodhouse Audubon. *John James Audubon*

c.1843. Oil on canvas, 35 × 27½″.
Courtesy, Department of Library Services,
American Museum of Natural History, New York.

*On the afternoon of November 6, 1843,
Audubon returned to his estate, Minnie's
Land, from his seven-month-long expedition along the upper Missouri River. Still
looking like a rugged frontiersman with
long hair and a full beard, he was greeted
by his wife, Lucy, his sons, John and Victor, and his granddaughters. John was so
impressed with his appearance that he
insisted that before visiting a barber
Audubon sit for his portrait, dressed in his
elegant, fur-trimmed, double-breasted,
green coat.*

Life mask of John James
Audubon

c. 1830 (?). Plaster.
Collection of The New-York Historical Society.

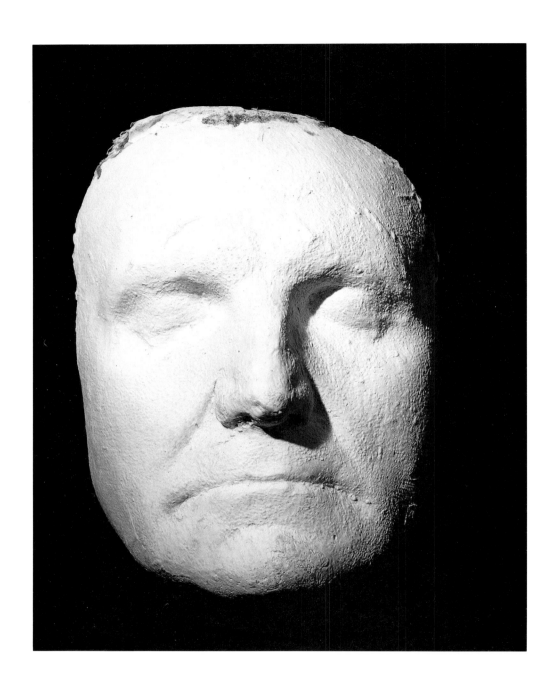

Davy Crockett celebrity to accomplish his promotional goals. With his long hair dangling on his befringed buckskin coat, the man of the wilderness regaled his drawing-room audiences on both sides of the Atlantic Ocean with Indian war cries and Ohio River songs, all the while eating raw tomatoes (then considered poisonous) and corn on the cob.

Life dealt a great many challenges to this complex man. Early in his career, he suffered a series of commercial setbacks culminating in bankruptcy. He endured the deaths of two infant daughters and the subsequent loss of two daughters-in-law, not long after they married his sons. Perhaps the most serious threat to his stability came from the very work that sustained him. In 1812, his portfolio of bird drawings, representing several years of work, was accidentally destroyed. He had carefully packed up in a secure wooden box (p. 122) all the drawings he had made to that date—about two hundred—and entrusted them to the care of a friend in Kentucky, while he traveled to Philadelphia on business. When he returned, he inquired after the box which was produced and opened. "But, reader, feel for me," he wrote, describing what he found. "A pair of Norway rats had taken possession of the whole, and had reared a young family amongst the gnawed bits of paper which, but a few months before, represented nearly a thousand inhabitants of the air!" (p. 123). His physical and emotional reaction was immediate and overwhelming. "The burning heat which instantly rushed through my brain was too great to be endured, without affecting the whole of my nervous system," he remembered agonizingly. "I slept not for several nights, and the days passed like days of oblivion." While this blow could have crushed his enthusiasm for exploring and recording birds, instead it spurred the resurgence of a will to survive and even to improve upon his loss. "The animal powers being recalled into action, through the strength of my constitution," he recalled, "I took up my gun, my note-book, and my pencils, and went forth to the woods as gaily as if nothing had happened. I felt pleased that I might now make much better drawings than before, and ere a period not exceeding three years had elapsed, I had my portfolio filled again."[99] It was the enterprise of discovering and drawing from nature that was both his inspiration and his salvation.

The complexity of the man, both his strengths and his weaknesses, is mirrored in the contradictions and quality of his work, both as a writer and an artist. He envisioned a grand scheme of penetrating the truths of nature in an original and accurate way. He set his own criteria for effecting a truthful image: first-hand observation of his subjects; precise reproduction of the original size; selection of a characteristic active pose. He invented new combinations of media, fabricated painting tools of his own design, and constructed special wire armatures to capture the fresh-killed colors of life. He refused to accept the handed-down opinions of authorities on natural history when they did not match his own observations. He despised and eschewed the traditional practice of working from stuffed specimens, whenever practicable. He spent years in the wilderness absorbing the sights, smells, and feel of nature in its pristine state through the passionate filter of his own perception. To accomplish this extraordinary goal, he also had to invent and create the man to do it.

Born illegitimate, he had to rewrite his past to erase the stigma of his birth and to surmount the insecurity it engendered. To compensate for a lack of formal art training and convince himself of his own abilities, he developed a fictional resumé of study with the great masters. Not descended from a scientific family, nor connected to learned societies, he promoted the value of direct experience over book learning as the proper practice of natural history. All the while, he was reading authoritative books on the subject to buoy up his observations with research. By the sheer "strength of constitution," combined with a passion and genius for the task, he worked diligently and created a unique contribution to the knowledge and representation of nature. Although he aimed to capture a new kind of accuracy, his goal was not the dry objective truth of the "closeted naturalists" whom he despised. It was nature "with life in it" that he set out to recreate on paper. He did achieve an unparalleled vitality in the work he produced; it reflects both the dynamism of the natural world he observed and the passionate inner world of the man who experienced it.

> *Was not the lost dauphin, though handsome was only*
> *Base-born and not even able*
> *To make a decent living, was only*
> *Himself, Jean Jacques, and his passion—what*
> *Is man but his passion?*

Robert Penn Warren, *Audubon: A Vision,* 1969

Notes

Chapter I.

1. John James Audubon, "Myself," *Scribner's Magazine* 13, no. 3 (March 1893): 267.
2. Edward H. Dwight, "The Autobiographical Writings of John James Audubon," *Bulletin of the Missouri Historical Society* 19 (October 1962): 26–27.
3. John James Audubon, "Account of the Method of Drawing Birds Employed by J. J. Audubon, Esq. In a Letter to a Friend," *The Edinburgh Journal of Science* 8, no. 15 (November–April 1828): 48.
4. John James Audubon, *Ornithological Biography, or an Account of the Habits of the Birds of the United States of America,* vol. 1 (Philadelphia: Judah Dobson, Agent, 1831): ix.
5. J. J. Audubon, "Account of the Method of Drawing Birds," 50.
6. John James Audubon, "Louisville in Kentucky," *Audubon Reader: The Best Writings of John James Audubon,* ed. Scott Russell Sanders (Bloomington: Indiana University Press, 1986): 27.
7. J. J. Audubon, "Myself," 284.
8. Edward H. Dwight, "Old and Modern Drawings: the Metamorphosis of John James Audubon, " *Art Quarterly* 26, no. 4 (1963): 462–463
9. Theodore Stebbins suggests convincingly that if Audubon was schooled in the French academic manner, it was probably by a follower of Jacques-Louis David at the Free Academy of Drawing in Nantes. Theodore E. Stebbins, "Audubon's Drawings of American Birds, 1805–38," *John James Audubon: The Watercolors for the Birds of America* (New York : Random House and The New-York Historical Society, 1993), 3.
10. Quoted in Dwight, "Old and Modern Drawings," 465.
11. John James Audubon, *Journal of John James Audubon Made During his Trip to New Orleans in 1820–1821,* ed. Howard Corning (Boston: The Club of Odd Volumes, 1929), 4.
12. J. J. Audubon, *Journal, New Orleans, 1820–1821,* 3.
13. J. J. Audubon, *Journal, New Orleans, 1820–1821,* 20.
14. *Ibid.*
15. Maria Audubon, *Audubon and his Journals,* 2 vols. (New York: Charles Scribner's Sons, 1899), 2: 77.
16. M. R. Audubon, *Audubon and his Journals,* 2: 17–18.
17. M. R. Audubon, *Audubon and his Journals,* 2: 108.
18. J. J. Audubon, *Journal, New Orleans, 1820–1821,* 48.

Chapter II.

19. J. J. Audubon, *Journal, New Orleans, 1820–1821,* 111.
20. J. J. Audubon, *Journal, New Orleans, 1820–1821,* 143–146.
21. John James Audubon, *My Style of Drawing Birds,* (Ardsley, New York: Published by The Overland Press for The Haydn Foundation, 1979), 17. Connections between Audubon's work and La Fontaine are explored in Amy Meyers, "Observations of an American Woodsman: John James Audubon as Field Naturalist," in *John James Audubon: The Watercolors for the Birds of America,* ed. Annette Blaugrund and Theodore E. Stebbins, Jr. (New York: Random House and The New-York Historical Society, 1993), 49–53.
22. *La Fontaine: The Power of Fables.* Exhibition of the New York Public Library, 1995. Co-curators, Paul LeClerc, Christina von Koehler, and Holland Gross.
23. Looking at nature as a repository of moral lessons for man was common practice in Audubon's day. In a review of Audubon's publication, *Ornithological Biography,* W.B.O. Peabody described an incident in which a Bald Eagle captures a fish from a hawk, having forced the bird to drop it. "Pity it is, that he should dishonor himself by such unworthy robbery as this," he wrote, "though it by no means destroys the resemblance between the king of birds and the

kings of men." "Audubon's Biography of Birds," *North American Review* xx (April 1832): 374.

24. J. J. Audubon, *Ornithological Biography* 2 (1834): 492–3.
25. J. J. Audubon, "Account of the Method of Drawing Birds," 49.
26. J. J. Audubon, *Ornithological Biography* 1 (1831): 324–325.
27. J. J. *Ornithological Biography* 3 (1835): 320.
28. J. J. Audubon, *Ornithological Biography* 1 (1831): 11.
29. J. J. Audubon, *Ornithological Biography* 1 (1831): 135.
30. William Swainson, "Some Account of the Work now publishing by M. Audubon entitled The Birds of America," *The Magazine of Natural History, and Journal of Zoology, Botany, Mineralogy, Geology & Meteorology*, 1, pt. 2 (London 1828): 49.
31. Benjamin Rowland compared Audubon's *Carolina Parakeet* with *Parakeet on a Blossoming Pear Branch* by a follower of the Emperor Hui Tsung (1082–1135) in *Art in East and West* (Cambridge, Mass.: Harvard University Press, 1954), 103–108.
32. Swainson, "Some Account," 48–49.
33. Alexander Wilson, *American Ornithology; or, The Natural History of the Birds of the United States*, 3 vols. (London: Whittaker, Treacher, and Arnot, 1832), 3: 335.
34. J. J. Audubon, *Ornithological Biography* 1 (1831): 160–161.
35. J. J. "Account of the Method of Drawing Birds," 48.
36. *Ibid.*
37. *Ibid.*
38. *Ibid.*

Chapter III.

39. Dwight, "The Autobiographical Writings of John James Audubon," 30.
40. *Ibid.*
41. Francis Hobart Herrick, *Audubon the Naturalist*, 2 vols. (New York: D. Appleton and Co., 1911), 1: 330.
42. William Dunlap, *History of the Rise and Progress of the Arts of Design in the United States*, 2 vols. (New York: Dover Publications, 1969), 1: 408.
43. Edward H. Dwight, "Audubon's Oils," *Art in America* 51 (April 1963): 78.
44. John James Audubon, *The 1826 Journal of John James Audubon*, ed. Alice Ford (Norman: University of Oklahoma Press, 1967), 356.
45. Waldemar Fries, *The Double Elephant Folio: The Story of Audubon's Birds of America* (Chicago: American Library Association, 1973), 5.
46. J. J. Audubon, *The 1826 Journal*, 356.
47. J. J. Audubon, *The 1826 Journal*, 252.
48. J. J. Audubon, *The 1826 Journal*, 356.
49. M. R. Audubon, *Audubon and his Journals*, 1: 153.
50. Susanne Low, *An Index and Guide to Audubon's Bird's of America* (New York: Abbeville Press, 1988): 10.
51. M. R. Audubon, *Audubon and his Journals*, 1: 175.
52. John James Audubon, *The Letters of John James Audubon, 1826–1840*, ed. Howard Corning (Boston: Club of Odd Volumes, 1929), 29–30.
53. M. R. Audubon, *Audubon and his Journals*, 1: 299.
54. M. R. Audubon, *Audubon and his Journals*, 1: 329.
55. A complete and thoroughly documented study of Audubon's first edition is Fries, *The Double Elephant Folio.*
56. John James Audubon, autograph letter, signed, dated London, 7 January 1835, to L. Reed, New York. Pierpont Morgan Library, New York.
57. Annette Blaugrund, "The Artist as Entrepreneur," in *John James Audubon: The Watercolors for the Birds of America* (New York: Random House and The New-York Historical Society, 1993), 37–39.
58. William Swainson's 1828 commentary published in Ann Shelby Blum, *Picturing Nature: American Nineteenth-Century Zoological Illustration* (Princeton, New Jersey: Princeton University Press, 1993), 107.
59. Quoted in Martina R. Norelli, *American Wildlife Painting* (New York: Watson-Guptill Publications, 1975), 61.
60. Quoted in Norelli, *American Wildlife Painting*, 61.
61. J. J. Audubon, "Account of the Method of Drawing Birds," 52.
62. Peabody, "Audubon's Biography of Birds," 404.

63. J. J. Audubon, *Ornithological Biography* 1 (1831): 32.

64. J. J. Audubon, *Ornithological Biography* 1 (1831): 31–32.

65. J. J. Audubon, *Ornithological Biography* 1 (1831): 503.

Chapter IV.

66. Stanley Clisby Arthur, *Audubon: An Intimate Life of the American Woodsman* (New Orleans, La.: Harmanson, 1937), 403.

67. Herrick, *Audubon the Naturalist* 2 (1911): 9.

68. J. J. Audubon, *Ornithological Biography* 3 (1835): 547.

69. J. J. Audubon, *Ornithological Biography* 3 (1835): 546.

70. Letter from J. J. Audubon to G. W. Featherstonhaugh, St. Augustine, East Florida, Dec. 7, 1831, quoted in Herrick, *Audubon the Naturalist* 2 (1911) : 12–13.

71. *Ibid.*

72. *Ibid.*

73. *Ibid.*

74. J. J. Audubon, *Ornithological Biography* 3 (1835): 383.

75. Kathryn Hall Proby, *Audubon in Florida* (Coral Gables, Florida: University of Miami Press, 1974), 18.

76. Carole Slatkin, catalogue entry in *John James Audubon: The Watercolors for the Birds of America*, 258.

77. John Wilmerding's "Winslow Homer's Right and Left," *Studies in the History of Art* 9 (Washington, D.C.; National Gallery of Art, 1980–81): 59–85, provides an in-depth study of this work.

78. J. J. Audubon, *Ornithological Biography* 4 (1835): 540.

79. J. J. Audubon, *Ornithological Biography* 4 (1835): 538.

80. J. J. Audubon, *Ornithological Biography* 4 (1835): 539.

81. Thomas Cole, "Essay on American Scenery," (1835) published in *American Art 1700–1960* edited by John W. McCoubrey (Englewood Cliffs, New Jersey: Prentice-Hall, Inc., 1965), 100, 109.

82. J. J. Audubon, *Ornithological Biography* 1 (1831): 31–33.

83. William Swainson, "Some Account," *Magazine of Natural History* 1, pt. 2 (London 1828): 51.

84. Philip Hone, *The Diary of Philip Hone 1828–1851* edited by Bayard Tuckerman, 2 vols. (New York: Dodd, Mead & Co. 1889): 1, 73.

85. F. H. Herrick, *Audubon the Naturalist* 2: 238.

86. *Ibid.*

87. Parke Godwin, quoted in F. H. Herrick, *Audubon the Naturalist* 2: 237.

88. John James Audubon, *The Imperial Collection of Audubon Animals: The Quadrupeds of North America*, ed. Victor H. Cahalance. Foreword by Fairfield Osborn (Maplewood, New Jersey: Hammond Inc., 1967), xi.

89. John Francis McDermott, *Audubon in the West* (Norman, Oklahoma: University of Oklahoma Press, 1965), 64.

90. Quoted in McDermott, *Audubon in the West*, 4.

91. John James Audubon, *Journal of John James Audubon Made While Obtaining Subscriptions to his "Birds of America" 1840–1843*, ed. Howard Corning (Cambridge, Mass.: Business Historical Society, 1929), 145–146.

92. J. J. Audubon, *Journal 1840–1843*, 70–71.

93. McDermott, *Audubon in the West*, 101.

94. McDermott, *Audubon in the West*, 10.

95. McDermott, *Audubon in the West*, 16–17.

96. McDermott, *Audubon in the West*, 19.

97. *Ibid.*

98. Quoted in Mary Durant and Michael Harwood, *On the Road with John James Audubon* (New York: Dodd, Mead & Company, 1980): 608.

99. J. J. Audubon, *Ornithological Biography* 1 (1831): xiii–xiv.

Chronology

1785   Named Jean Rabine at birth, John James Audubon was born at Les Cayes, Saint-Dominique (now Haiti) to Captain Jean Audubon and his paramour, Jeanne Rabine, who died six months later.

1788   Voyaged to France with his father to settle in Nantes and be raised by his father's wife, Anne Moynet. The couple adopted the boy and named him Jean Jacques Fougere.

1803   At eighteen, Jean Jacques traveled alone to the United States to manage his father's Mill Grove farm at what is now the village of Audubon, near Norristown, Pennsylvania.

1805–6   Returned to France for a year. Made pastel drawings of birds which he gave to his fiancée, Lucy Bakewell, on his return to America.

1808   Married Lucy Bakewell, daughter of William Bakewell of Fatland Ford estate near Mill Grove.

1809   Son Victor Gifford Audubon born in Louisville, Kentucky.

1809–19   Merchant, mainly at Henderson, Kentucky. Son John Woodhouse Audubon born in 1812. Two hundred of his bird drawings were destroyed by rats. Two daughters were born and died. His business failed and Audubon was forced to declare bankruptcy.

1820   Employed as a taxidermist at the Western Museum, Cincinnati, Ohio. Decided to draw and document all the birds of the United States for publication. Embarked with student assistant, Joseph Mason, on boat trip down the Ohio and Mississippi rivers.

1821–24   Taught drawing, tutored, and painted portraits in Louisiana to support gathering of bird images. Lucy and his sons joined him.

1824   Visited Philadelphia in unsuccessful effort to get support for publication devoted to birds. Returned to Louisiana to raise money for trip to England to find publisher and subscribers for *The Birds of America.*

1826   Audubon met warm reception in England, where he raised money and gathered contacts through the exhibition of his bird paintings. William H. Lizars, an Edinburgh engraver, agreed to publish *The Birds of America.*

1827–29   London engraver Robert Havell replaced Lizars as publisher. Audubon visited Paris. Gained acceptance in European scientific circles by presenting papers at the Wernerian Society.

1829   Returned to America and painted birds in the northeast with backgrounds provided by the artist George Lehman.

1830   Began work on *Ornithological Biography* with William MacGillivray as scientific editor.

1831   In Charleston, met John Bachman and established close family ties that would last the rest of their lives. Traveled through Florida—to the St. John's River, Indian Key, Sandy Key, and Key West—painting and documenting birds.

1833   Accompanied by son John, traveled to Labrador.

1838   Engraving of all four folio volumes of *The Birds of America* completed. Five-volume *Ornithological Biography* completed the following year.

1840   Started work on *The Viviparous Quadrupeds of North America* and on the smaller, octavo edition of *The Birds of America*, lithographed by J. T. Bowen of Philadelphia.

1842   Audubon family moved to their Minnie's Land property on the Hudson River, at what is now West 155th Street and Riverside Drive in New York City.

1843   Summer expedition with friend and naturalist Edward Harris and assistant aboard steamboat on Upper Missouri River region. Octavo edition of *The Birds of America* completed.

1847   Audubon suffered a stroke, followed by increasing mental incompetence.

1848   Last of three-volume *Quadrupeds* completed.

1851   Died at Minnie's Land on January 27, age 65.

1886   First Audubon Society founded by George Bird Grinnell, a former pupil of Lucy Audubon.

Selected Bibliography

ADAMS, ALEXANDER. *John James Audubon: A Biography.* New York: G. P. Putnam's Sons, 1966.

ARTHUR, STANLEY CLISBY. *Audubon: an Intimate Life of the American Woodsman.* New Orleans: Harmanson, 1937.

AUDUBON, JOHN JAMES. "Account of the Method of Drawing Birds Employed by J. J. Audubon Esq. F. R. S. E. In a Letter to a Friend." *Edinburgh Journal of Science* 8(1828): 48–54.

AUDUBON, JOHN JAMES. *Ornithological Biography, or an Account of the Habits of the Birds of the United States of America, accompanied by descriptions of the objects represented in the work entitled The Birds of America, and interspersed with delineations of American scenery and manners.* 5 vols. Edinburgh: Adam and Charles Black, 1835.

AUDUBON, JOHN JAMES. *Journal of John James Audubon Made During his Trip to New Orleans in 1820–1821,* ed. Howard Corning. Boston: Club of Odd Volumes, 1929.

AUDUBON, JOHN JAMES. *Journal of John J. Audubon Made While Obtaining Subscriptions to his "Birds of America," 1840–1843,* ed. Howard Corning. Cambridge: The Business Historical Society, 1929.

AUDUBON, JOHN JAMES. *The Letters of John James Audubon 1826–1840.* 2 vols. 1930.

AUDUBON, JOHN JAMES. *Audubon's Birds from the Original Water Colors in The New-York Historical Society.* New York: Hastings House, 1946.

AUDUBON, JOHN JAMES. *The Bird Biographies of John James Audubon,* ed. Alice Ford. New York: Macmillan Company, 1957.

AUDUBON, JOHN JAMES. *The 1826 Journal of John James Audubon,* ed. Alice Ford. Norman: University of Oklahoma Press, 1967.

AUDUBON, JOHN JAMES. *The Imperial Collection of Audubon Animals: The Quadrupeds of North America,* ed. Victor H. Cahalane. Foreword by Fairfield Osborn. Maplewood, New Jersey: Hammond Inc., 1967.

AUDUBON, JOHN JAMES. *My Style of Drawing Birds.* Introduction by Michael Zinman. Ardsley, New York: Overland Press for the Haydn Foundation, 1979.

AUDUBON, JOHN JAMES. *Audubon Reader: The Best Writings of John James Audubon,* ed. Scott Russell Sanders. Bloomington: Indiana University Press, 1986.

AUDUBON, JOHN JAMES, AND REV. JOHN BACHMAN. *The Viviparous Quadrupeds of North America.* 3 vols. New York: Published by V. G. Audubon, 1845–1848.

AUDUBON, MARIA R. *Audubon and his Journals.* 2 vols. New York: Charles Scribner's Sons, 1899.

AUDUBON, MARIA, AND JOHN JAMES AUDUBON. "Audubon's Story of his Youth. 'Myself'." *Scribner's Magazine* 8 (March 1893): 267–289.

BOLGER, DOREEN, MARC SIMPSON, AND JOHN WILMERDING, eds. *William M. Harnett.* New York: Harry N. Abrams, Inc., 1992.

BLUM, ANN SHELBY. *Picturing Nature: American Nineteenth Century Zoological Illustration.* Princeton, New Jersey: Princeton University Press, 1993.

BURROUGHS, JOHN. *John James Audubon.* Woodstock, New York: The Overlook Press, 1987.

COFFIN, ANNIE ROULHAC. "Audubon's Friend—Maria Martin." *New-York Historical Society Quarterly* 49 (January 1965): 29–51.

DAVIDSON, MARSHALL B. *The Original Water-color Paintings by John James Audubon for The Birds of America.* New York: American Heritage Publishing Co., Inc., 1966.

DOCK, GEORGE. *Audubon's Birds of America.* New York: Harry N. Abrams, Inc., 1979.

DUNLAP, WILLIAM. *History of the Rise and Progress of the Arts of Design in the United States.* Reprint of 1834 edition. 2 vols. New York: Dover Publications, Inc., 1969.

DWIGHT, EDWARD H. "The Autobiographical Writings of John James Audubon." *Bulletin of the Missouri Historical Society* 19 (October 1962): 26–35.

DWIGHT, EDWARD H. "Audubon's Oils." *Art in America* 51 (April 1963): 76–79.

DWIGHT, EDWARD H. "Old and Modern Drawings: The Metamorphosis of John James Audubon." *Art Quarterly* 26, no. 4 (1963): 461–479.

DWIGHT, EDWARD H. *Audubon Watercolors and Drawings.* Utica, New York: Munson-Williams-Proctor Institute, 1965.

FORD, ALICE. *Audubon's Butterflies, Moths, and Other Studies.* New York: Studio Publications, Inc., 1952.

FORD, ALICE. *John James Audubon.* Norman: University of Oklahoma Press, 1964.

FORD, ALICE. *John James Audubon: A Biography.* New York: Abbeville Press, 1988.

FRIES, WALDEMAR. *The Double Elephant Folio : The Story of Audubon's Birds of America.* Chicago: American Library Association, 1973.

GERDTS, WILIAM H., AND RUSSELL BURKE. *American Still-Life Painting.* New York: Praeger Publishers, 1971.

GOPNIK, ADAM. "A Critic at Large (Audubon's Passion)." *The New Yorker.* February 25, 1991: 96–104.

HARRIS, EDWARD. *Up the Missouri with Audubon: The Journal of Edward Harris,* ed. John Francis McDermott. Norman: University of Oklahoma Press, 1951.

HARWOOD, MICHAEL, AND MARY DURANT. "In Search of the Real Mr. Audubon." *Audubon Magazine* 87 (May 1985): 58–119.

HARWOOD, MICHAEL, AND MARY DURANT. *On the Road with John James Audubon.* New York: Dodd, Mead, and Company, 1980.

HAYDEN, ARTHUR. *Chats on Old Prints.* London: T. Fisher Unwin, Ltd, 1906.

HERRICK, FRANCIS HOBART. *Audubon the Naturalist.* 2 vols. New York: D. Appleton and Co., 1917.

HERRICK, FRANCIS HOBART. Introduction to *Delineations of American Scenery and Character,* by John James Audubon. New York: G. A. Baker and Company, 1926.

JAMES, EDWIN. *Account of an Expedition from Pittsburgh to the Rocky Mountains, performed in the years 1819,1820. By order of the Hon. J. C. Calhoun, Secretary of War, under the Command of Maj. S. H. Long, of the U. S. Top. Engineers. Compiled from the notes of Major Long, Mr. T. Say, and other gentlemen of the party, by Edwin James, botanist and geologist to the expedition.* Vol. 1. London: Longman, Hurst, Rees, Orme, and Brown, 1823.

KEATING, L. CLARK. *Audubon: The Kentucky Years.* Lexington: University Press of Kentucky, 1976.

LINDSEY, ALTON. *The Bicentennial of John James Audubon.* With chapters by Mary Durand, Michael Harwood, Frank Levering, Robert Owen Petty, Scott Russell Sanders. Bloomington: Indiana University Press, 1985.

LOW, SUSANNE M. *An Index and Guide to Audubon's Birds of America.* New York: Abbeville Press, 1988.

McDERMOTT, JOHN FRANCIS, ed. and comp. *Audubon in the West.* Norman: University of Oklahoma Press, 1965.

MILES, ELLEN, ed. *Portrait Painting in America: the Nineteenth Century.* New York: Universe Books, 1977.

NORELLI, MARTINA R. *American Wildlife Painting.* New York: Watson-Guptill Publications, 1975. Published in association with the National Collection of Fine Arts, Smithsonian Institution, Washington, D.C.

PEABODY, W.B.O. "Audubon's Biography of Birds." *North American Review* xx (April 1832): 364–405.

PROBY, KATHRYN HALL. *Audubon in Florida.* Coral Gables: University of Miami Press, 1974.

REYNOLDS, GARY. *John James Audubon & his Sons.* New York: Grey Art Gallery and Study Center, 1982.

ROGERS-PRICE, VIVIAN. *John Abbot in Georgia: The Vision of a Naturalist Artist.* Madison, Georgia: Madison-Morgan Cultural Center, 1983.

ROWLAND, BENJAMIN, JR. *Art in East and West, An Introduction through Comparisons.* Cambridge, Mass.: Harvard University Press, 1954.

SITWELL, SACHEVERELL. *Fine Bird Books, 1700–1900.* New York: Atlantic Monthly Press, 1990.

SLOTKIN, RICHARD. *Regeneration Through Violence: The Mythology of the American Frontier, 1600–1860.* Middletown, Conn.: Wesleyan University Press, 1973.

ST. JOHN, MRS. HORACE. *Audubon, the Naturalist of the New World, his Adventures and Discoveries.* Boston: Crosby, Nichols, Lee and Company, 1861.

STAFFORD, BARBARA M. *Voyage into Substance: Art, Science, Nature, and the Illustrated Travel Account, 1760–1840.* Cambridge, Mass.: M.I.T. Press, 1984.

SWAINSON, WILLIAM. "Some Account of the Work now publishing by M. Audubon entitled The Birds of America." *The Magazine of Natural History, and Journal of Zoology, Botany, Mineralogy, Geology, & Meteorology* 1, part 2 (1829): 43–53.

WARREN, ROBERT PENN. *Audubon: A Vision.* New York: Random House, 1969.

WELCH, MARGARET C. *John James Audubon and his American Audience: Art, Science, and Nature, 1830–1860.* Ph.D. dissertation, University of Pennsylvania, 1988.

WILSON, ALEXANDER. *American Ornithology; or, The Natural History of the Birds of the United States.* 3 vols. London: Whittaker, Treacher, and Arnot, 1832.

WILSON, EDMUND. *Patriotic Gore: Studies in the Literature of the American Civil War.* London: Andre Deutsch, 1962.

Index